small rain

small rain

Eight Poets From San Diego

D. G. Wills Books
La Jolla, California

Library of Congress Catalog Card Number: 96-60298
ISBN: 0-9651267-0-6

Editor:	Kate Watson
Book Design:	Bob Dickson
Cover Design:	Greg Calvert, Artifax, San Diego

Published by D. G. Wills Books
              7461 Girard Avenue
              La Jolla, CA 92037

Western wind, when wilt thou blow,
The small rain down can rain?
Christ, that my love were in my arms
And I in my bed again!

Anonymous

Contents

Page

Richard Astle 1

Asymmetry 3
from Inside the Brain Museum 4
  Nights of Wine and Blankness 4
  What No One Would...Live Through Twice 5
  Picking Up Speed on the Offramp 6
  Driving in the Dark 7
  Want What You Have 8
Half Life Begins at 40 9
Cowboy 13
The Decay of the Vacuum 14
from Suite Punk Violins 22

Sarai Austin 23

SHIRTS 25
Missouri Mules 32
She was a big woman... 34
THERE IS A SONG WHICH MAKES ME THINK THIS: . . . 40
She... *(an excerpt)* 41

Ted Burke 47

Lunch Money................................ 49
Making the Best of the Love Lost Between Them .. 51
Ed Rusha of Oklahoma Lives in Los Angeles 54
Language of Joy 56
Three Dream Meditations 58
Down Time 61
From the Top of Your Head 65
No Use Crying 67
Double Nose Dive 70

Peter Dragin 75

Lament for My Mother 77
Comes the Season Opener, My Dad Is Gone 79
Moses and Schizotheism 80
There Are No Alternative Fuels 82
Bidding Adieu to My Teeth 84
Charlie Speaks of Travel 86
Phenomenology of Spirit 88
Hearth of Silence, House of Mortality 91
A Map of Secret Murder 93
A Short History of Love and Strife 95
Goodbye to Berlin 98
MEMOIRS...SCHIZOPHRENE LIBERATION FRONT ... 100

Paul Dresman **103**

Introduction: How Poetry May Be Useful 105
Orientation 107
Traveling Through Centuries 110
It Will Compose Itself 111
Under the Arch 113
The Case 115
Theatre d'Resurrection 117
Eros 118
Everything Composite Is Transitory 120
The Omega 127

Patti O'Donnell **129**

Postcards From a California Winter 131
A Rhododendron Blooming 133
Lyric Suite 135
Urban Nocturne 139
From the Language Cage 141
Outside Utopia 144
Untitled Spring 146
Friday Afternoon at the Zoo 149
Emily, Sometimes You Scare Me 151
Where the Music Ends 152

Bonnie Rosecliffe **155**

Surprised by Morning 157
Outburst, 5:00 A.M. 158
The Dream Is Love 160
Just As 162
Bhajan 163
Polishing the Silver 165
No Stone God 167
Piece for Two Hands 168
The Limits of Language (or the uses of words) . . . 169
Blackbird 172

Kate Watson **179**

Caterpillars in Hawk Canyon 181
The Depression, 1931 183
The Immigrants: Where the Roots Grow 185
Boundaries 186
Trinity 188
The Clachan 189
Smudge 193
The Waterfall 194
A Patient Master 196
Into Silence 198
For a Refugee Boy...in Bosnia 200
Solo 202

About the Poets **203**

Richard Astle

Asymmetry

A man stands at a screen door. It is night.
His eyes jerk twice for headlights as they reach
a corner that is just within his sight
that turns towards her. The screen divides his fea-
tures into little squares, a pixeled look,
his stance is leaning forward with his eyes,
his hand goes where his ache is. You could brook
a pun and call him digitalicized.

A love that travels nowhere, everything
ecstatic stops. Stops and starts. The end
recedes from sight, from memory. We bring
our absence with us, like the dead
moon in the room we slept in when
nothing mattered.

from Inside the Brain Museum

We never lose the past, we just accumulate.
            —Joe Jackson
You've got to deal with the real.
            —Iggy Pop

Nights of Wine and Blankness

You ask me for advice, I say, "Use the door."
            —C. Hynde

Coming off another one, those nights
of wine and blankness, waking up,
the memory of a telephone that bites
the fingers on the buttons. That sad pup
his midnight madness made him. Now he sits,
a cigaret in bed, two round blue pills,
a notebook and a pencil, as he fits
his feelings into lines, attempts to fill
another frame inside the brain museum,
remembering her voice but not the words,
he contemplates the loneliness of freedom,
listening to the morning song, the birds
of memory, of love, of tedium,
and roughly trims his toenails with his thumb.

What No One Would Want
to Live Through Twice

Keeping plants alive, now there's a trick
requires attention, water, pluck of leaf;
to rearrange my room means I am sick,
and smoking means she's gone. There is no grief
worth living for. By television light
my feet make shadows on this text;
inside the brain museum late tonight
your face against the wall. A Sominex
at bedtime. Tales we tell
about our days in destiny's small cell
are stories only. Living is a shell
of condensation, face against the knee,
a cage of meaning, narrativity,

what we don't contain is poetry.

Picking Up Speed on the Offramp

These are your cigarets, this is her champagne,
This is the end of the world this endless year;
Introjection's working here,
A way to cut the loss and start again.

Unless you're still here, looking over her shoulder—
"Imperializing my space." Well,
there's nothing like a little bit of hell
to let you know how fast you're growing older.

Some of these days don't seem quite real.
You wander in a white dress through my dreams.
The brain museum bathed in light.
Sheets on fire, ocean breathing steel.
Everything's exactly what it seems
to be tonight.

Driving in the Dark

What's going on here anyway? I say
you don't have to send me home, and you
say Thinking clearly you're not. What to do
but walk right out, imagining a day
where nothing be but us, a brief respite
inside the brain museum, your green eyes
"impossible," a rush to love, surprise
among some ruins in our lives.
                                            Yes it
is more and less than memory.
                                            Last night,
behind your car, my headlights dim,
you warned me at the freeway's rim
then pulled away, your taillights bright
red stars slowly fading in the left lane;
red stars fading slowly in the left lane.

Want What You Have

The easy life is over—
Look out now, I'm coming over.
—Thomas Parke D'Invilliers

I know it's impossible but still I
want that moment before desire comes
crashing up on very daily life
and strands us in the brain museum.

A dream of innocence disguised as lust
but this is not that big one, this is just
a story told before the story's told.

While we talk our tales grow cold.

We've gone through everything, around the block
more times than dogs. The land of dreams
has left us. Love, let's walk
hand-in-hand down twisted streets
with no more future, mindless luck,
and nothing to repeat.

Half Life Begins at 40

1. There's a gap. He is writing a story, then he's here, the wind in the window.

2. Something is being constructed. The one in the middle. Narration makes a message out of yesterday, last year. Oh do not say "what is it." "He wanted to write a story with four characters, a man and three women." Stop making sense. He *was* writing a story, then he's here, the wind in the window.

3. A glass of wine and memory. Your face upon the wall. We write our stories backwards as we live. But there's a gap. Is this what he wants? No. It is tomorrow.

4. Something is being constructed. "We made it for a while, then we stopped. Life goes on." Someone brings the bodies home. "I love the smell of napalm in the morning." Ten years ago, twenty, tomorrow. There is no description, only life against the wall. We played with each other. Is life too pleasant here in this hotel? We took it seriously. Now helicopters make me think of you. Vina, Berkeley, Vietnam, Del Mar.

Something was being constructed, but not anymore.

5. "He thought perhaps he should just begin to write, end these hesitations, let his writing determine where his characters would go." Rewriting stories backwards as we live. Had they too much in common? Would they get into trouble, miss each other, waiting in a station for a train already gone? Or is that old hat already?

There IS no understanding, only words in line.

6. Ten years ago, at this cafe, a man hung up his briefcase telephone, arose and drove his Porsche into a wall. Why does this story make me think of you? Nothing is alike, but that doesn't explain.

One face fades into another, trip ticket, triptych. Who is the one in the middle? You, me, someone I knew before, someone I'm meeting now. Stop making sense. Who would we be if we knew who we are?

7. The story makes a V, a wedge, a triangle against the scene. "What really happened." A point of intersection, perspective of a railroad track. "I don't know how to come on anymore." Then the drifting apart.

7a. The story, written backwards, makes a V, that myth of origin, that dream in chains. "The story's brick wall is that sudden abandonment may be a part of the fiber of our lives today, and that fairness has nothing to do with it." Where would we be if we knew where we were going? "We make our stories to explain ourselves." Badly.

8. "By the time the harvest moon crossed the chicken wire, Richard had looked at his life and was ready for a new one." Imagination takes his breath away. Stop. There is no tomorrow, only yesterday and now. Something is being constructed however. Something to be desired. He dreams. *That's* what he keeps inside and does not count.

9. Politics or poetry, life against the wall. We live our lives in practice for another. Are all our stories versions of other, real, stories?

There is no life, no wall between us, sitting on the fence of disillusion, waiting for an end that will not come, or will, or has, who cares this morning, sun in this cafe, this corner table, this shade, that bird, this book, this pen, this hat, this cup of coffee third refill, voices in the middle distance...

"'Literally I've said what I've had to say. Even if there was anything more to add, I'd keep it to myself. That's how things are. There's no absolute yes and there's no absolute no. I'm sitting here, with you now, but I might easily not be.'"

10. "like the Balinese say 'we have no art, we just do everything as well as possible.'" He thinks about the time he leans across her, out into the night. White wicker room. No, it is sunset, a winter Friday afternoon. He hears helicopters overhead. It gets dark. Out to sea a boat is burning. A sight that, if he hadn't

really seen it, would be symbolic. The burning meets
the waterline and goes out.

thanks to t. s. eliot, robert duvall, sheila benson,
thomas mcquane, acker/genet, tom raworth,
david byrne, steven rodefer

Cowboy

Various words excite you
Not what I'd expect
Camel, zebra, bear, and gnu,
Doctor, architect;

A combination I find odd,
But then you're passing strange;
My words: mountain, stove, and sod—
My home is on the range.

The Decay of the Vacuum

*...better than a half-dead cat
in a box. —William Jordan*

The morning sun replaces Sunday night. Across the
street a red car meets the curb. Doors open, a breeze
of language. On the right a scene already described.
A one-night stand is fun and sometimes not. A sen-
tence doesn't fit. Where gull meets buoy. Halluci-
nates a whine outside the window. The subtraction of
the background remains a significant source of
uncertainty in the results of any experiment. Oh joy
of language, dream of publication. Somewhere in the
air an angel wings. It's time to go to work.

The beach here is too crowded in the summer.
She prefers it in late fall, those weeks of cold and fog,
hands in parka pockets, seagull's call. The collision
itself, however, is a violent process, in which appre-
ciable energy can sometimes be transferred to the
electrons, raising them to excited states, so that
lower-lying orbitals are temporarily vacated. She
often wonders if she'll meet someone there, different
than a summer meeting, souls out for solitude find-
ing each other.

The vacuum is ordinarily defined as a state of absence, but no more. One might expect that the vacuum would always be the state of lowest possible energy, but one would be wrong. In the quantum field theories that describe the physics of elementary particles the vacuum becomes somewhat more complicated. Experiments are now under way.

I always thought it was "under weigh," as when a ship lifts anchor, somewhere on the seas to meet—what?—the absence of nothing against the waves, experience, land, the lapse currently on a long run in the culture, another ship, mermaids.

He walks past her house when he can, though it is out of his way. Sometimes he sees her through the window, but she doesn't see him, so he doesn't wave. The repulsive force between two nuclei, which results from their electrical charges, grows rapidly as their separation is reduced. There is something self-ful about his distance, as though it means something, he can't say. The nuclei remain within the critical range only for a period that is considerably shorter than the average decay time of the neutral vacuum. Later, when he learns she knows what he's doing, he'll stop. This does not mean the decay cannot take place at all.

Another page goes into the machine. It's all the same, absence of the new. Various recurrences; or, it's all random. The last sentence will be the following:

Indeed, the agreement is close enough to inspire confidence that the decay of the neutral vacuum will soon be detected. It's not the last sentence yet.

He walks past her house every day, or as often as he can, though it is a little out of his way. That's it, faking uncertainty, changing facts in mid-stream. Thatta ploy. Repeat when necessary to maintain continuity. He walks past her house when he can. Now that it's winter he can tell if she's home by the light. What time is it?

What would happen if Z could increase without limit?

He thinks of another time, years ago, a woman he met at a party, impulsively kissed upon a balcony, not hers, he didn't even know her, she was with someone else, she gave him her phone number, there were trees next to the balcony, he grabbed for a leaf and got needles in his palm.

Pair creation wd be singalled by the appearance of the positron, wch wd be expelled from the atom and cd be detected w/ a suitable insturment. The spontaneous appearance of such a pair is not furbidden by any conservation law. If events a dis kind cd be observed under ideal conditions they wd hav a simple apairance. At this pont the theorie begins to make ambigruse perdictions, whose interpenetration is uncertain.

One thing, twice, another thing—repetition. The decay of the neutral vacuum cannot take place instantaneously.

If the electron is removed from a hydrogen atom, the result is a stable neutral vacuum, which will persist indefinitely as long as the electron is not restored. After a while her boyfriend claimed her, felt her up, and took her home. Repeat, when, necessary, to, maintain, continuity.

For strong fields, predicting the state of a single electron invariably becomes a many body problem. After she left there was nude swimming in the pool. When the charge of a bare nucleus first exceeds the critical value, two positrons should be emitted. He didn't enjoy it like he wanted to because he cdn't wear his glasses in the water. These extraneous positrons represent a distracting background to the events of interest. An old lover, her clothes in a distant bedroom, wanted help when the cops came, but they came just for the noise. The nucleus itself is often prompted to an excited state and can return to the ground state by emitting a photon. He swam underwater on his back.

The vacuum near an overcritical charge is a vacuum that cannot be emptied. Things keep coming out that weren't there before they left. Like cats in the cupboard, in the bag, in the night.

He called her up; she said she wanted to fuck. He didn't question her too closely, checked his ears. Was *he* an object of desire? How did *that* happen? He took her out to dinner. That's how he did it those days. The Otherbird Cafe and home to his waterbed. Between, she said, "I didn't expect dinner."

1) He walks past. He doesn't look. 2) He walks past. He glances around, looking for the house, sees her, pretends not to. 3) He waves, doesn't slow down. 4) He says, "Oh, hi. I forgot you live here." Does he expect to be believed? Is this a game? 5) He says, "I was going to say, 'I forgot you live here,' because I didn't want you to think I was walking by on purpose." What purpose? This gets complicated. 6) "But if I said that," he adds, "you'd think I planned to, a clever ruse." What does she think of how much he's thought to say? 7) The speaker vanishes. "I'm glad to see you anyway." They fuck.

A couple of hours later she wanted to go home. She said it was worth it; he still hadn't figured her out. She went back to her boyfriend, a bit longer. He called her a couple of times, then called it a one-night stand.

Place one thing next to another, tying time together, producing sense in the folds of it. Repetition rises. That's what it's for. Incantation. If I sit here at the same table, drinking a similar beer, at the same time of day, the same thing might happen.

Never mind that it's not the same day of the week, and that the sun stays up, already, noticeably longer. Spring (and all). Two beers this time perhaps, then home to write this fantasy.

It is at this point that the neutral vacuum becomes unstable and the charged vacuum appears. Is this the process of pair production? Particles created in this way have only a fleeting existence: they are annihilated almost as soon as they appear, and their presence can never be detected directly. They each took something from it, something that wasn't there.

Repetition, that's the thing. The same acts in the same order to the same end. Allowing for certain differences, *that* can't be avoided. "Don't send me home," he says, as his hand slips in, thinking, Now.

The plot thickens, or tries to. The story becomes a statement—"Life has meaning! Narration makes sense!" Descartes creeps out of the classroom, a horse passes, then silence. He walks past the house again. Is something about to disappear?

They won't meet, or if they do it will be a mockery, a moment in Marrakech. Someone goes to Rabat to teach the king's son freshman composition. A used care salesman turned collage professor, he knows where his bread lies. Will he be the one to meet her, to take her off that beach, after all?

Do his friends like it when he uses them like this? Do some like it, others not?

Something out of nothing, the self, an other. She notices otherness in his eyes, or he in hers, but doesn't know what to do with it. Is this some kind of love story? Meanwhile he's getting writer's cramp, this ballpoint pen, no table to lean on, and even with the keyboard, rewriting later.

Is this a road to romance, a substitute for it, or defense? Ah writing! Ah desire!

Is this the vacuum, and the charge between?

When she stands on the beach now she sometimes thinks of him, and of her first attempt to break away from a man she didn't know why she'd tired of. He thinks of her when he's horny and alone.

During heavy-ion collisions the binding energy of the electrons of the innermost orbitals rises steadily as the distance of closest approach is reduced and the electric field becomes more like that of a single overcritical nucleus.

Not what either of them expected. Did they *both* act badly? Repetition might have strained a space, a vector towards some future. But it wasn't that kind of thing, not ever. So how could they expect what they did not get?

Creating the world in our own images: no one is who you think. I *mean* you.

Or is it "*Whom* you think"?

"If she believed what he believed her to believe…"

Years later, a walk along those cliffs again, sight of a short-covered ass down a hillock, he walks to the front of the cliff, staring down, a V of surfers against a wave, she can see him, he knows, and think she's not seen herself. Moments later, after a quick glance back punctuates a stare at the sea, he turns, walks past her, south along the cliff, and sits. They're partially in sight, he hopes she notices. They both stare, no doubt, at the sea, write things down. Later one will say to each other, "Come here often?"

Although no unambiguous evidence for the decay of the neutral vacuum has yet been recognized, we can still find a way to weigh anchor on the slipsloppy ship of the future. Let us all have happy endings. The agreement is close enough to inspire confidence that the decay of the neutral vacuum will soon be detected.

thanks to l. p. fulcher, j. rafelski, & a. klein

from Suite Punk Violins

and then you find you're in a novel, not reading,
the plot is all around you, characters
with complex motives, counterpointed stares,
and violins, like fishes, slowly breeding
scenes no one would want to live through twice.
Young love is in the alleyway, quite drunk
with hate and death. Nobody here is punk.
The heroine solicits your advice,
the villain gleams, his fangs revealed at last,
and moral clarity becomes a sport.
It's melodrama not great fiction you meant.
And while you pause, anticipate denouement,
meaning rides the narrative impasse,
and poetry becomes the last retort.

Sarai Austin

SHIRTS

When I asked you to leave
I hadn't realized this meant
you would take your shirts,
shirts I have lived with for years
they had become somehow mine,
the shirt your mother criticized
the laundry over for leaving the collar soiled,
and this years before the commercial
(and my coming into my own with laundry).
That was the shirt with the thin,
blue lines that matched your eyes.
The summer we met you had
a favorite red-striped shirt.
You wore it almost every day
and I liked that sort of loyalty.
The one I bought to replace it
didn't work, as replacements never do.
When I asked you to leave
I hadn't realized this meant
you would take your shirts.

Shirts I have lived with for years,
shirts I have washed on the normal setting
because I did not like the concept of synthetic,
shirts I have ironed with my General Electric
Shot of Steam 'til they were
crisp and smooth to touch,
shirts I have slipped on after making love,
smelling of Right Guard, and darker hair, and
other subtleties I didn't know
how to appreciate,
shirts I have buttoned and unbuttoned,
shirts I have cried on and hugged,
shirts I have clung to and ripped up for rags,
shirts I have mended and loved,
the short-sleeved shirt you wore to the river,
the shirts you grew up to
when you wore a business suit and tie.

I always wanted to dress you in blue,
learning your neck size,
the length of your arms;
shopping for you because you never would;
shirts imported from England,
dark blue Madras from India,
embroidered shirts from Pakistan,
shirts with button-down collars,
shirts that open down the front
with no collars at all.
You tell me I always gave you

the best shirts,
you haven't had a good one in years.
I was very wrapped up in your shirts,
when I asked you to leave
I hadn't realized
you would take them with you.

Today another man is leaving.
Once again I have overlooked
the implications,
the loud rustle of shirts on hangers
walking out the door,
breaking my heart harder than ever,
realizing the importance,
the necessity of shirts,
these shirts I have fought with
refusing to wash and iron them.
And he too was a man loyal to his shirts,
wearing them way past their time,
shirts I have folded and put on the chair,
not letting them into my closet.
Now the closet is almost unperturbed
but how empty the chair is from this terrible loss
of shirts to hold.
Only last week when everything else was gone
I mended his button,
washed and ironed his shirt,
this red shirt I bought for St. Valentine's,
breaking my heart with its loud sound

walking out the door.

You come to see me,
I tell you once again
shirts have left my life.
You are wearing a blue t-shirt
with a pocket over your heart.
I cry, not telling you
how I wanted to call
when the shirts walked out the door,
how much I needed a safe, old shirt
when it started to hurt,
hearing the sound of shirts leaving.
I wipe my eyes on the shirttail
of the work shirt I have gotten
from the man who has just left
with his shirts.

I have always liked inheriting your shirts,
the new ones I buy never work,
I like the old ones I get from you,
all broken in and full of life,
your favorite one I rescued
after you used it to wash the car,
the green Western shirt
you threw away because it ripped,
the pink one I bought too small
telling you I should have it,
you didn't look good in pink.
I see how I have tricked myself,

sneaking your shirts back in.
I feel like I should bury them,
erect a monument in the backyard
to your shirts, but this is hard to do,
this final severing with shirts.

I need to sing a song to shirts:
shirts made of velour with
elk horn buttons from Montana,
shirts opened down the front,
shirts worn with the sleeves rolled up,
shirts made of cotton, shirts made of silk,
shirts that men work in and are loyal to,
shirts that men wear to play like little boys,
shirts that mothers send, all wrong,
because they never know their sons as men,
shirts from Salvation Army,
Saks and Saba's Western Store,
shirts with gold braid and flashy buttons,
shirts made of khaki, corduroy or flannel,
shirts that are sheer,
shirts that are strong,
shirts that women care for
as a high act of love,
shirts from India, Korea and Pakistan,
shirts that make long journeys
to find the right man,
shirts you can see through,
shirts that are soft to touch,

shirts that smell and taste
of the man you know,
shirts that come home to you at night
and wrap a collective 66 inches
around your 24-inch waist,
I need to sing a song
to shirts I have sought
and shirts I have let go of.
I need to sing a song
to shirts I have cried over
and touched and loved.

It used to be I wouldn't sew shirts.
They had French seams, collars and cuffs,
buttonholes and other complications.
There were too many difficulties
involved with shirts.
But now I need to sew a shirt
made with delicate hand stitches
from cloth that three million
silk worms have died for,
a shirt that requires learning
a new handicraft, performed with care,
a shirt with engraved buttons
and hand-stitched openings,
a shirt with silver trim
from an heirloom wedding dress.
I need to sew a shirt with patience
and love that startles the sky.

Everywhere I walk I see shirts.
In the supermarket, by the dairy case,
the little boy's t-shirt
with the big red heart saying
"I love you, Dad," hurts me so,
I have not bought milk in weeks.
The man in line, I study
the yoke of his shirt,
shirts that whisper in the morning,
shirts stretching across broad shoulders,
hanging from skinny backs,
shirts making a statement,
weary in the world of commerce
where they are never touched,
shirts that burp babies,
shirts that saw trees,
shirts that have so much to do
that are treated so haphazardly,
shirts I would fight for,
shirts I would protect
shirts I would keep home with me,
shirts I would care for and cry over,
shirts I would love so hard
it would shock even the sky.

Missouri Mules

Faulkner insisted on raising mules rather than cattle. It possessed, he recalled, a built-in principle of retirement, and so resisted the most entangling of alliances: "Father and mother he does not resemble, sons and daughters he will never have."
> —William Faulkner: His Life and Work
> *by David Minter*

i

My daddy raised mules. Missouri mules, I suppose. I think this one little piece of information has a lot to say about my life. Stubborn as a mule was an often used phrase. All contradiction, any assertion of will, fit within this broad category.

ii

My sister's best friend was born with a defective palate, so she always talked funny. She was my parents' favorite and I suspected the handicap helped a lot. The only thing that could come close to a cripple was somebody dedicated to simple-minded obedience, who didn't just do it out of necessity, but actually believed it.

Hunsakers owned a store in town. Mr. Hunsaker kept bees, among other things. When they tore down the grade school, he bought up all the desks, chalkboards, and everything else he could carry away.

Mrs. Hunsaker finally got sick of his junk and put up a big sign in the front yard that said CITY DUMP. Mrs. Hunsaker was the only woman who, not just once, but on a regular basis, called her husband a horse's ass.

I don't remember for sure, but I think she died young.

She was a big woman...

It's a weird place I know, but I can always be amazed
by it. On any given summer Sunday somethin' can
happen that looks just like it stepped out of a Diane
Arbus picture book of Appalachia. The sort of thing
you'd think must have been captured and locked up
on paper at least a hundred years ago, the unstated
underbelly of the place that makes it so haunting,
that gives everybody born there some story to tell if
they can ever figure out what it is, the contradiction
that is so fused into life as to be almost the founda-
tion of the culture. It's never talked about, nobody
even seems to notice it, which leaves it free to work
its way into you, like a worm in an apple. Plain lives
go by day by day, undisturbed by things that would
have more sophisticated folks sittin' up and pointin'.
Here it's no more than somethin' to swat at, like a
gnat or a bothersome mosquito.

We were sittin' there in the backyard by the
smokehouse in those S-framed metal lawn chairs left
over from the fifties, the ones that were almost
always painted green and bounced just a little bit

once you got it down how to get 'em goin'. Daddy's Uncle Jim was just gettin' down to the good part of one of his train stories about takin' the train for the first time as a young man—a train to Minnesota, or a train to some war, or a train to work somewhere out of the fields. Where the train went exactly was apt to change from Sunday to Sunday, but a train story is a train story and about as good a way as you can get to pass away a Sunday between mornin' preachin' and evenin' prayer meeting.

CLICKETY CLACK that same old train
is takin' him back
clickety clack   clickety clack
comin' back

There was usually a place in there where he worked in somethin' about the only girlfriend he ever had and buyin' her a diamond

CLICKETY CLACK   CLICKETY CLACK
her bein' gone when he got back
CLICKETY CLACK   CLICKETY CLACK
same old train comin' down the track

and Uncle Jim's too old to notice anyway how many times he's told which stories and how much they shift from Sunday to Sunday, Daddy playin' with his little John Deere lawn tractor, his wife showin' me somethin' in a crochet book, my daughter takin' pictures of woolly worms with her Kodak instamatic.

We were sittin' there in the lawn chairs, with the gnats and mosquitoes, and train stories and woolly worms, when this couple came walkin' up from the dirt road that ran alongside the extra house out back. I didn't really see them come from there but it's a reasonable explanation for their appearance. Though it seemed to me like God had just sort of opened up the bean fields and these people arose, some earthbound, wingless birds reborn as poor folks to remind us who we were, to show us our own desperate mortality as some sort of Sunday lesson, to remind us despite trains and clocks to control the spending of time, that no matter the clickety clack, the rhythm with which we spent our time, clocks and trains and time would stop.

She was a big woman walkin' in front of the man. I must say my heart almost stopped when I looked up at her, she looked so much like one of those photographs of Mama in the twenties, in the days before they made whatever they ever did make, when the stories have it they had a three-legged table nailed to the wall to hold it steady. That is just about the only time I ever liked, those three-legged table days I never saw but only heard of in old stories. My heart almost stopped, thinkin' "Good Lord, it's Mama walkin' by, the way she would, just to check on what's happenin' with me here so close to home."

She was a big woman walkin' out in front of the

man, in a man's shoes too big for even her large feet. Her legs were strong, unshaved and dusty from the trip up out of the earth. She had a stern face and high cheekbones just like Mama's and the same sort of flat twenties hairdo that had never been done. Her hand-me-down clothes hung on her large frame like Mama's did when her health started to fail, like bleached sheets on the clothes line, movin' with the breeze.

It was a Sunday in the high nineties in the month of August with no movement but the gnats and mosquitoes. She was a big woman walkin' in front of the man across the backyard toward the smokehouse and S-framed metal lawn chairs, which I do believe were painted green. She was a big woman lookin' 'em in the eyes, askin' could they please spare a cold drink of water, inquirin' was the little house out back up for rent. Daddy's wife answered, "No, it isn't," Daddy said there was a hydrant by the shed if they wanted a drink. She was a big woman headin' off to the highway, while Daddy's wife assured all of us she'd "rather rent to a nigger for sure than trash like that." It struck me like lightnin' she could have been my mother, but for a tiny turn of time and luck, my mother's life could have been the same. She was a big woman. I could picture her in that photograph of my mother in white, fashionable summer shoes with high heels and thin straps, a design in the mesh of birds in flight, that photograph which first made me appreciate my mother's great legs, one leg thrown over the other, her arm flung on the back of one of those S-framed metal lawn chairs, me in a ruffled pinafore, pickin' up woolly worms from the grass. Mama sittin' there in some smart, summer frock, sure of her life and sure of herself.

She was a big woman headin' off toward the highway, covered in dust, her throat full of hot water, and all I could think was, she could have been my mother. I could see her as a lady, dressed in crisp, white cotton and smart shoes. She was a big woman—with the courage she moved across the lawn to ask for a drink and the dignity with which she bent down to sip from the spout as though it were as gracious a way as any. She was a big woman, walkin' out in front of the man. I couldn't help thinkin' she could have been my mother.

Uncle Jim went right on with his train story, while Jana recorded the woolly worm for comin' generations. I, for one, was just as destroyed as I ever had been by this place where people can be treated worse than dogs just because they're poor.

She was a big woman, walkin' out in front of the man toward the highway goin' further south. God knows why. Uncle Jim was on diamond rings; Jana was learnin' to predict winter weather from the color of the woolly worm. I was silent while my heart screamed, but no one listened. She could have been my mother. She could have been me. She should have been a lady—she was such a big woman. I was silent, hidin' out behind my *Portable Faulkner*, which I couldn't hardly get into, considerin' the circumstance—catchin' a line from his speech for receivin' the Nobel, somethin' about the human heart in conflict, how the poet's voice can help man endure and prevail, and I couldn't help thinkin'

there but for time and trains
goes my mother, my self
these earthbound, wingless birds
sprung from a fissure in the fields,
moving across the scorching earth
asking for water.

We go on asking for water.

THERE IS A SONG WHICH
MAKES ME THINK THIS:

I would have liked a balalaika for breakfast,
in the garden after sleeping late.
A table of pink wrought iron leaves and frosted glass,
our milk poured from a sheer green pitcher,
bowls of black cherries and cream.
Your hands smoothing the placement,
curling the napkin,
a yellow tanager in the pepper tree.
My foot on yours beneath the table/
while we consider the morning and plan our day.

I should have liked all this,
YES
and a balalaika.

She... *(an excerpt)*

Here is bare woman. Hair pulled back. Her face newly washed. She sees Venus, with one arm reaching toward heaven, take shape in the bubble bath. A pointed-toe shoe. She rubs her body with the rough towel, briskly around her ears, to the back of the neck, between the breasts and under them. Here is bare woman. Learning to be brave in silence, looking for a new way. A voice talks to her in the tub saying ritual gives form. She wants to expand it to "Form defines meaning." It is a natural habit to complexify, a habit she has taken on from her world. But she reminds herself, "The new way is not a way." She is learning which voices to ignore, to know when she is veering off the path which is truly her own.

She is digging down through the layers of her life, searching for the pulse which is steady, which can be sustained and is sustaining. Her solar plexus like the vegetable garden she is trying to create outside her kitchen door, she unearths bulbs from other seasons, chunks of cement, the fierce roots of a thousand weeds. She works with her hands slowly in a Zen attention. Pulling her ribs open to ease the breath.

Shin is a whisper in the room. Spirit. Here is bare woman digging, digging softly into her life, into the flesh of her soul. Her fingers rubbing needlepoint flowers, learning the way she knows how to, by touch, through feeling. She places her fingertips upon her lips in a very deep quiet. New leaves, folded closely on the freshness of their life take shape on the rose bushes she has just brought home. Here is bare woman, looking for a woman's way. Do means way. Here is bare woman without make-up or high heels, unsure of the books she has read.

She sees herself dressed in white. Cleansed of the men who have violated her. It is a cleansing she does not know how to accomplish, except through the constant vigilant seeing of it. She wants to bless the moist muscle of her whole being, to take it back from all the wrongful hands who have touched her without seeing. She wants to give a soft circular motion back to her hands. To treat them as more precious than gold, to choose carefully what she puts her hands to.

She wants to take up her feet and gently rub the calluses away, undo them of the bitter burning of Caesar's path, which they have had to harden themselves to. She touches the place where she imagines her ovaries to be. She folds her legs in half lotus in her desk chair, and scratches the hollow of her cheek.

She pushes firmly on the solar plexus point, she opens to her life. She prepares to make it her religion.

She finds herself in the same world that you and I occupy. The common one. The one where the pursuit of a biodegradable cleaner is sometimes our high act for the day. The world with cat stains on the carpet and children with a greenish-colored snot. The world which has taught us deadly habits, to clean and order the life out of our lives. The one which has taught us to wait until the children are sleeping, until the dishes are washed, until the laundry is folded, until our husbands are out of town, until the bread is baked, the yard is weeded, until everything is finished and there is nothing left, to find a way to bring ourselves into the way we are living our lives. The world which has taught us to be afraid to confront the silence, the bare space between our hip bones, the emptiness we feel when the men and children are gone and there is nothing to clean.

She begins to see her feet as sacred and to be careful where she steps. She holds her hands in the little Zen circle she has learned, a twinge pricking the lower chamber of her heart and asks someone to take a photograph so she can remember herself. She is determined to stop squandering her life. She challenges the world for her right to open the curtains on what she is really doing here, gathering pebbles for her vision of a large stone wall. She challenges the world for her right to open the curtains on the life she is really living, where some days she weeps and cannot make the carrot juice she is committed to drinking. She dances across the room in an old pattern that is different now, placing each foot with a firm gentleness out from her body. She whistles, although she does not know how to.

Here is bare woman. Her life pared down on purpose, in order to be rid of the distractions which prevent her from living her life, bereft of men and children and sinks to clean. She fingers her way to the center of the bloom, to the moist middle where pistol and stamen can live in harmony. She learns the way she knows how to, through touch, by what her hands tell her is true. She closes her eyes and lets her fingertips tell her the vibration of red, the necessity of texture. She comes to appreciate the rough places on her face.

Sometimes she wants to line the symbols of her life across the floor, the feathers and lace, to touch them one by one in order to teach herself who she is. Small green stones placed in a circle of sand. Hot pink fans. Pear decals and floral paper. There is nourishment—and fire she must relearn. She lets her belly be as round as it is capable of and contemplates fullness. She puts away the music that men have given her and confronts the silence. The palm frond outside her window inaudible in its motion. She learns to go within to claim dominion. Here is bare woman. No paint upon her face. Nothing to hide behind. Unmasked. Revealed and revealing.

Weary of deceptions and distractions, looking for the revelation of her life. She uses scents to hold her where others' arms have failed, breathing in the musk she rubs on her wrist, her room smokey with sage. She stirs the ashes. In a sweeter mood she chooses tea rose sprinkled heavily down her skin like so many petals. She sees herself kneeling prayerfully to the East before the parsley she has just planted. She does not know why, but the vision persists.

She watches her breath, a sudden angular lurch through her body, now a wave breaking repeatedly upon the cliffs of the interior of her abdomen. A figure eight circling around and around itself. She walks the alleys of her life looking at the piles of garbage, empty flowerpots stacked against fences, worn blankets crumpled in cans, blackened soup pots stuffed in boxes, last year's city directories blowing open in the breeze. Here is bare woman trying to re-find her own rhythm, fingers to her wrist hoping to feel pulse. Recognition gives authority, she says, squinting her eyes, hoping to see herself.

Here is bare woman. She weeps because life is too precious to touch, and she lives through her hands. She fingers her beads. She aspires to the greatness in the day-to-day, to the divine in the dishwater, the eternal in the cat fur, the transcendence of her own hair.

Ted Burke

To my parents

Lunch Money

The way to stop
what kills an appetite
is a lesson
school menus
eluded to in all
the course descriptions
of Home Ec.
and Auto Shop.

Lunch was three
puffs of a cigarette away
behind
the bungalow
where the band
stashed the instruments,
all that dented brass
rusting in closets
whose coat hooks
could put an eye out.

There was never a
course in sand,
even though

sand is coarse, of course,
which was probably why
there were no classes
at the beach,
though it is funny
that all I ever learned
was her name
after I got her shorts
off
and discovered
a school of thought
that had no walls,
but acres of campus.

Making the Best of the Love Lost Between Them

Woe begone in song
of the violinist
wandering around tables,
annoyed as he bows
the neck
at
the haircuts that bob
and shake fists
to his melody and tale
of two Black Forest lovers
beset by a pack of wolves.

Bristles are the cuts
on the head of the throng,
he bristles himself
and often longs
for a seat
nearest the podium,
starting the night off right,
a tempo to signify
the romance of his moods.

Yet his songs are too sad
for his present crowd,
they like it in chords
that blast and clash
the anger of gods
they can't even name,
their rhythm is violent,
not suited
for violins
and the sentiment they exclaim.
The kids want to see Industrial Cities
slip into Great Lakes
as backdrop
for a riff
on the E Major scale.

Yet they're all stuck,
they by blizzard
and he by hunger
and the need to eat,
and they make the best
of the love lost between them.

They sit, listen, gnash their teeth,
and he plays frantic cadenzas,
dreaming of applause and bows,
of tuxedos
and ladies in long, white gloves.

And together

they make
music that's
jagged and
dirty.

Ed Rusha of Oklahoma Lives
in Los Angeles, California

Awestruck
in mystery landscapes
that are bubbles
on my tongue,
language
I've always seen,

No comments
on airless rooms
where the smoke
hasn't shifted,
windowless
with walls
facing terraced valleys
where Industry
gets deeper
and hopelessly lost.

We choke
on the choice
of corollaries.

I've seen
these gas stations
and the brand names
of Los Angeles
explode
a hundred times before
where the desert
used to sleep.
Your eyes have me
canvassing the county
for a hundred of our years.
I find myself in another man's socks
humming to the static,
we'll play with the A.M. radio when the music fades
and everything
gets too close to call.

Language of Joy

Speaking of times in twangs of alien regions which share memories of months and distant smells of dust and oil rising from the black asphalt hours before the rains came.

California is the vat of raw alloys where grandchildren meet each other in jobs that make no sense and compare notes over black, tasteless coffee about what it was their grandparents were saying, something in code that firmed up their backbone and brought mists to their eyes.

We are too many years past the expiration dates of our lives to think of parachutes when it's Autumn by the Pacific Ocean, in a city whose best boasts are sand, gunboats, warm air and cool breezes that turn us into a generation of rasping sighs in lawn chairs nursing drinks under tourists' umbrellas in the neighborhoods we moved into three decades earlier in expectation of making a mark on a locale of fronds that was as unknown as anything we wanted to do with our lives.

It's about gloom and rain and love of defeated weath-
er that is a tempest we brave going out the doors of
our homes.

It's about being sorry for the rich for being so pathet-
ically well off when integrity is the only thing on the
menu.

In bars in motels near county fair grounds,
dealing with degrees of English and slants of the
camera's eye, it's about the loneliness of standing in
the same place long enough to see prodigal sons and
daughters come home with news of the war, a sinking
feeling that gunboats are not enough.

Wondering what in the universe makes sense when
you're bored beyond despair, and philosophy is now a
cable channel broadcasting into the clouds until
everyone returns from the beach,
from the water
of laughter from rivulets that come
in many streams,
the language of joy.

Three Dream Meditations

1.

I dream a life without covering my eyes, you and
I can see the legends of the map,
there are no stories, yet dreams of waking hours
have their facts, it's about you and I seeing what
hasn't been believed or excused as wives' tales or
                        bachelor bragging,
we confront condominiums armed with coat sleeves,
I see around the corners of all arguments, I am
                        Elastic Man,
a life dreams of us in stiff back chairs,
                        taking notation, tapping
pencils to spiral wire, seeing us in Hell before
                        courage becomes
the mere act of licking the stamp and thinking of
                        revenge in Editorial cartoons,
you are Elastic Woman, strained over rhetoric and
                        stretch marks.

2.

I dream a smile you had facing a window thick with
the grease of the fries we were eating there over
coffee drinks near Shattuck, you stared through the
                    streaks of grease
and vapor to traffic lights rioting on the corners and
                    intersections
transmitting contrary codes of behavior to car high
                    beams scarcely
lit or aware of messages being sent, yet staying in
                    their slick portions
of road, you were crying and mentioning miracles
                    and migraines, tobacco
smoke swirling around your head in gray,
                    punctured halos, you said
the lights were pretty and artful and the
                    smudges on the
window made them seem like streaks of paint whose
                    violence of color, whose
explosions of tone resembled something we recognize
                    only after it's broken,
whose parts are guts of larger parts blurred and rapid in
                    spinning directions
of every twist of enemy gravities. I watched you get
                    misty for what used
to move somewhere and who used to move it, you're
                    moving
me to tears, I said, would you like me to move in?

3.

We come here dreaming of ruined gardens and
                        terraced hillsides
with their ghosts of Architecture amd tastes,
I used to imagine the world was full of love as long as
Elvis could dream,
it really is this simple,
just tell me "I know what you dream by that,"
which means I'm going to kiss you now,
long and deep
and probing into
the valley of dreams
where I have never and forever walked
picking dreams from trees blooming
in unknowable colors and tints,
I am going to kiss you and take you and lie down
with you on beds of grass
that are humbled
by our dreams of rain.

Down Time

Your life was in boxes
that day you toughed
out the flu
and someone
named Brewer
brought you a burger
to the pantry door
that was the end of bragging
in your usual bed.
Tom ate
rice cakes,
running his hand
across the back of his
neck, reading Zen
as you
watched the streets
where it never rained
drown in downtown
tears about
the flow of cash
stopping when Heaven

tosses a fit.
Karen kept crossing streets
until something
gave out,
the spines of the books
she'd read and the men she'd bedded,
and all she gets
to do is dance.
You're busy being an adult
in the thick of your
pages,
snapping your neck
to regain your wits.
It could be that the phone is tapped,
and it could be
no one cares
how many lines
you've written since
they threw dirt
on Kennedy
and gave him
a fire no cigar smoker
has yet cozied up to.
It's raining downtown,
the signs are
smears in the eddies
of the petroleum products
our wars are paved with.
Brewer and Tom

have met for coffee
and Karen
calls it a night with a ream of paper
and Smith-Corona.
Somewhere you
think of
women you won't
name
and get lonely
all over again and cough in scooping
heaves of the chest
that shift lodes
and light a cigarette with a wooden match,
head in water beads
and listen to
the lunatic in the rain
outside your window
screaming at God,
calling him all his secret endearments,
his eyes inches from the crack
in your drapes,
the skyline shakes,
the last bus leaves,
bartenders check their key chains,
the ocean boils in layers,
your head burns
and your cigarette
is killing you,
you wonder what

she's been doing,
you listen
to the
night.

From the Top of Your Head

From the top of your head
flowers grow that I've never seen
in the nature of my asking
the meaning of this thing,
so beautiful, the wind.
The wind in all uses highlights
the shift of your hips
leaning against rocks,
the meaning of this,
the earth,
the mother of the deals
that have us eating out
of hands that pick the roots
of your hair
that goes on growing like flowers
on hills with all the houses
we've never lived in.
A clap of thunder is
applause enough for pausing
to smell the turpentine
that revives the hem and haw

of the wood under our shoes,
rainy nights are ovations
and the trance
of still looking into your eyes
where I've always seen them,
on pyramids, in circles,
thirsty yearning.
From my hands comes ruined meaning
about hammers and nails
and the holes that made them,
I've stared at your face
on the ceiling all night,
water flows where there is no resistance,
insistence makes me forget
and remember your names,
every center has a heart
and every heart is broken.
Into your face
all roads split down the middle,
the wind is a whisper and a rustle of notes
coyotes cry
in the wake
of our
progress,
so beautiful, the wind,
and water rolling
in circles, in circles, in peace.

No Use Crying

Wouldn't it be the dumbest luck
to see you coming
across a parking lot,
arms full of groceries,
shapeless sacks sagging
under the corners
of milk cartons and canned goods,
waving at me against the
sun and the witness of
a store sign nailed to
passing outbreaks of sunshine,
calling my name,
smiling, out of breath,
hands negotiating groceries
and untied laces crossing
your path over the measured asphalt,
calling me with
your eyes sending signals
of "Wait for me,"
and "How long has it been?"
and "Remember me?"

All this just when
I've gotten into the car
with my friend Mike,
who's driving,
and who's three days
without a cigarette
and in no mood to
stick around
because there's nothing to do
with his hands anymore
except drive,

All this when I see you running to the car,
you seeing me see you,
Mike's car at the exit
two seconds before
he makes a right turn
sharp as teeth
into thick traffic
that races into perspectives
of abstract congress,
me not saying anything to Mike
and watching you
in the rear view
drop your groceries, sacks tearing,
your hair and American flags blowing the wrong way
                    in the wind,

Me thinking of love that might
have been
sadder than it happened
if I had never stopped drinking,
honestly glad
that today
wasn't the day I had
to talk to you,
'though I am sorry about your milk,
it spilled so large and white and cold.

Double Nose Dive

Living in shambles and gambling
on luck
when the moon
is over the Cove
and lights the coast
with gray radiation
that spooks each
crag and crest
with half-light and full life
I felt
after loving you in
a bush
that was older
than the city that owned it.

I was forever lost for words
that were the remains of
breathing and my glasses
steamed with vapor
as I tasted you
in a valley
where your valley
was always wet

and wild as nose came
finally to nose and
salt air
preserved every sting
and stain of
getting our clothes off,

You take my breath away
climbing trees,
grabbing branches
your tongue glistens
and chances a
taste of the root
that is limb and
life of metaphor and limber
in manner
of babble and sounds
that come from us,
echoing
miles up
the coast in reaches
of beaches
where no army
has known return fire,

I am climbing mountains
where God
had all his good ideas,
I am pedaling uphill
in a clutch of fingers

pulling me in,
I am strength
that ebbs and passes
to where strength
needs to be,
your mouth finds
my ear
and you bite me
when the moon allows,
when those stars, really suns and spinning
              complexities of life
              that begin and end somehow,

get closer
than sheets in
military beds,
you said my name
a dozen times
and I only grunted
the names of gods
that were only grunts
and cracks
 and a rime of light just
licking the horizon
where water meets
black tarp of sky
and I see nothing to return to,
no life to come back to
except

sleep

and maybe your
breasts
where my head
would rest
and your heart
would beat
in rhythms
that are
as history of music
suddenly understood
no matter
how much or how long
we stammered
on the drums of our tongues
getting to
know each other's
names
when life around
melted away
and there was nothing
but each other's eyes to
read.

Living under a moon
near a coast
with the shredded
raincoat

of ghosts
who've stopped knocking,
tonight
there's only
knocking,
another inland room
in another city
designed for passing through,
knocking,
trembling walls,
a rime of light,
knocking.

Peter Dragin

Lament for My Mother

Gulls
blown inland:
migration
begun,

they stream south,
break and wheel,
rise slowly,
cyclonic, and
break
    again,
high and distant
into a fluent
stream south.

Love,
last week
for the last time
I kissed you.

Your soft hand:
ashes on
a tender sea.

Light of this
mid-November
afternoon:

delicate,
mysterious
surrender to

the kiss on the wind
from before
anyone ever was cold.

Comes the Season Opener,
My Dad Is Gone

The last moon of the rainy season
has waned and passed weeks ago;

my nights run late with work and worries, and
I could use a touch of rain upon the window.

Daybreak will come. High spring. The wind at dawn
will warm quickly, move everywhere at once,

the pigeons on my balcony will coo and strut
their safe and shady nest together twig by twig,

and I will sleep and search the colors of my dream
for help: a year since I kissed your brow, and

your eyelids closed. Jupiter tonight is fierce
among all the stars, our house is a shell unsold.

Past, future, your absence everywhere at once,
this tea, cool comfort, bathes my grieving tongue.

Moses and Schizotheism

On another planet
the schizophrenes
are dominant:

I greet you both eight times,
once each for each one
of the two of you,

once and again
from the couple
I comprise.

Not a crowded planet
but densely woven
with conversation,

the great thing being
that hugs and kisses
among these people

never actually end
but roam mental galaxies

like episodes of
I Love Lucy

ever vivid,
crossing deep space,

laughter, kin of light,
a constant.

Their constitution
is written in
lilies and orchids,

they adjudicate
by the dance
of bees in clover;

leaving no tracks,
they save the whole price

of contracts, suits and appeals.

And when it comes time
to go to war,

after checking it out
for an aeon or two,

they decide that since they all
outrank each other,

everyone's orders
are canceled,

and nobody's absent
but they all enjoy their leave.

There Are No Alternative Fuels

We are all in all afloat
in the empty space
of our atomic flesh:

presence once arrived
greets presence
ever arriving

in the house
made of heat;

in the forest's
hospitality to
the rising sun's light,

in prime ordered
stillness and silence

where birds wing and
make song as they warm

dwells the work.

Each compression and expression
of lips, teeth and tongue,

imagine it makes one dawn,

imagine the brain's measure
in vibrant silence and heat;

we are all
Ancient in Days, so

tell me what you could
possibly want
from torching the Amazon,

the rape and mutilation
of every family
tribe and nation on earth:

what's your pleasure?
A car of your own?

Bidding Adieu to My Teeth

A lotus:

veins iridescent
sap dancing with light

from the quickly
shadowing root to

the petals
breaking surface

full blown
on the stratosphere:

a thunder cloud
twenty-five miles across and

beyond
mother father teacher

beyond
trance path fruit

where sits
a Buddha

in bliss of
emancipation
arrived at

by the way
in all the vast wind
simply of surrendering:

rain for our thirsty forms,
and the empty heart in the hail.

Charlie Speaks of Travel

a favoring wind
for Karen

Lunar composure
back-lighting the eyes,

dazzle sliced with shade,

nubile
calico cat

pausing
for my grateful fingers

not twenty feet
from the stream
of enameled tonnage,

the voltage uncounted
along La Jolla Blvd.,

offers her fur
blessed in fish oil,

proud as a panther's,
and especially the ear

quick as silver and
sweetly she insists

the way it runs
this tide can never be turned

to hamburger.

Phenomenology of Spirit

Trills and pipings,
bar fragments

in the higher reach
of the flute's register

filtered through the glass
of the balcony door

I am cleaning
from the outside,

first the gross dirt
then the streaks and
then a swipe at clarity.

Once I knew a woman,
an historian,

who signed her
saturday evenings

over to the cause
of cleaning my lover's
house and minding

two brilliantly
active toddlers

(my lover's
and her own)

while we
went to the movies:

sweeping apace
the trail of their
luminous rumblings

she attended to
toilets, ovens,
all the major tasks,

and bore
with diplomatic
aplomb

the critique

of dust
left on doorjambs,

the streaks
on mirrors and windows;

silent as a mafioso,

she took the rap
for breakage

and what was missing
from the fridge.

I step inside
my house again

to the revelation
it was Couperin
all along,

a stately
orchestral blues;

and it's true
labor too
has its chordal

structure.

Hearth of Silence, House of Mortality

Boneache of tedium,
the toll a faint heart exacts;

like scraping sand from granite,
this drawing breath
from the fortress wall of the wind.

Isolated, inarticulate
after years of watching my
loved ones slowly fall dead;

labors, dreams, embraces
imbedded like small missiles
of glass in the brain,

my blood sits down
at the feet of the rain:
the yoga that forgives fever.

If I say the wind is heavy
can I say that matter's light?
Any scout makes fire from flint;

freeway traffic amounts to
the detonation of A-bombs
diffused, usefully spent.

Maybe it's malignant, this lump
of fear that I carry; and this may be
the last you ever hear from me,

my swan's wings beating through
some semiotic dusk.

But I doubt it:
once I saw a spirit crowd
of war dead tumbling

down a pre-dawn sky
and through my bedroom window.
The news from heaven is good:

there is no news from heaven.

A Map of Secret Murder

Dawn light of my crime;
dread skims the glassine

rippling skin of the ocean of all
that I am ever likely to see.

Fish of my intentions,
Beware! You will gasp

from the bone, a fire rising
that would eat what your

pleasing meat can not know:
the wish to kill. This solar blood

sinks its stain into
clouds, storefronts, friends,

astonishes the wind which
stops, shivers, starts again.

Oh blood blown into meat and bones,
what do they want with me,

your tidal, kneading fingers?
And what is this that I am thinking?

And this I know: I haven't stopped
breathing yet, and
have not yet, and have not yet…

A Short History of Love and Strife

Tonight
the humblest

of our local
independent stations

presents Nick Nolte
in Nicaragua

and just
when the battle's beginning

my screen goes nuts
with the radiations

from the helicopter
circling over our houses

in the service of law
and security.

By interference
the electromagnetic

sea becomes
a political economy

shifting and pitching
under
the witnessing moon.

Has it really been
ten years and more?

Will it be
ten years, or more?

Tonight
I will risk the street

and search the tavern

as the dedicates
of friendliness
worldwide do,

searching the faces
in song and in dance

joined to
the current

of

timely and timeless
celebration

of

the declaration

of

uncanny
intercontinental

dignity and peace.

Goodbye to Berlin

Sitting and standing alike,
all of us eager for

neighborhood and home,
a packed bus at quitting time.

A seat opens up, and I, weary scholar,
sit down gratefully beside a junkie

who spies the title of my new bought book:
Kiss The Hand You Cannot Bite,

and wants to know
what it is and what it's worth:

an essay in vulturous hygiene gone mad,
a history of the Ceausescus.

"Good study," he says, and we ride a bit
and he talks about it.

"Junk knows: history repeats itself,
tubers of Africa, corn of Mexico..."

when his vision fixes on
the Asiatic belly of the former Soviet Union,

how it warms, sweated and moving beneath
the northering sun this time of year.

East San Diego, five o'clock light in April,
commerce washed in waves of recession

that lick in a tide, up the boulevard
where custom fades, wasting under threat of arms,

my friend gets off at 35th, and I at 59th,
thinking, film you might see again,
                but never your dreams,

and who speaks of commerce as custom
anymore. It's the summary end of the 20th century,

where you can get your head blown off
                just walking around,
and in Berlin, in the '20s,
even the perfume was called *Decline Of The West*.

MEMOIRS OF MY SERVICE
IN THE
CONTRA-INTELLIGENCE
SECTION OF THE
SCHIZOPHRENE
LIBERATION FRONT

by Ashley Phoenix

Chapter 1: Rendezvous and Recruitment.

She is not Control, therefore
she issues no order,
but she confuses the enemy
by contradiction three ways to heaven and beyond.

My lady complected of lights more fine than rainbows,
serving your aspiration, venturing bliss, this night I am
would no more pad his expense account
than you would your fine cotton, dancing bodice.

Not our mission, I know,
but what fine will they ever levy
so to posit finally an end
to all imposition?

Polymorphous spirituality!!!

Beryl faced, dream bodied angels of Erotic Justice…

Apocalyptic perversity!!!
Super-nova flesh of Compassionate Rage…

May an interdisciplinary conference convene,
a court of boogee woogee last resort,
the wisest of whales and eleephumps,
the primate, vulpine and apian nations,

to take a finding, considered and concluded,
as to whether our symbolically decorated
syntactical warps actually mean anything,
or can ever, before it's too late;

"Well, I'm ready for Freddy," my father used to say,
in apparent reference to Mr. Sand Man;
but we could never be sure unless he yawned first,
those yawns that would shiver the very windows and
                    timbers of our house.

The Elements press their etheric appeal
down at the Palace of Real and Divine Laws:
*These hominids be doofusses, come on
God, you gotta do **something**!*

And that's the name of that old tune:
the pass of her passionate whisper
troubling the face of that dark, dark wine
that day of the strange rendezvous

over a table made of cedar, marbled with stains,
with the library behind us at last speaking in
                    tongues of flame.

Scroll and codex and book deliver
their vapors up to a refractively pleasuring,
                    maternally reaching sky;
and hive-dry ash settles where the middle sea
                    would lull by wave swell and break
would rock the tormented body of knowledge
                    back to sleep.

She called it the eye in which heaven and earth
                    see single;
she called me the pupil within which all heaven
                    and earth does see.

She crossed my tongue with fool's graciousness;
ah, the permanent pink slip of my recruitment,
memory fresh as the daisy this day is,

Consuming and nourishing as her arms ever are,
with and in sweet Alexandria....

Paul Dresman

Introduction:
How Poetry May Be Useful

I took an open truck from Lhasa to Chamdo, a three-day trip, but it took ten. The truck kept breaking down, and we ran out of food. We bought a yak and cut it up. You get to prefer parts of the yak. Some parts are better than other parts. There are parts I actually like because they're raw. Then there's the fact that you can't cook yak in the back of a truck. The roads were bad. We got bounced around. Then we would break down again. It was like a song or a New York novel. Somewhere between here and anywhere, we blew part of a head gasket. There were no spares, and there was no cork, not in Tibet, not on the road to Chamdo. So I volunteered the cover of my anthology of *Great Poets Under Forty West of the Eastern Divide.* It's a classic. Duly cut to shape, it fit the head and off we went again in the truck across Tibet. At a pass over seventeen-thousand-foot mountains, the truck began to slide on some ice. The entire distance, the Tibetan pilgrims had chanted *Om Mani Padme Aum,* and I had gone along, chanting with them. But at that moment when the truck slid slowly toward the edge of the pavement,

the shoulder, the cliff, and all the Tibetans sped up
their chant, I switched to the Lord's Prayer. I had just
started to say "Our Father who art" when the driver
must have jammed it in reverse. The tires caught on
gravel. We stopped. The truck was rocking. The
engine had died. You could hear the kind of low whine
the wind makes in high passes, and I realized we had
all fallen silent, standing, looking down into the abyss.

Orientation

I discovered one way to orient myself,
I went to work in China
while the character I had been
stayed home in the singsong of the open American
        road,
going nowhere, drinking gasoline, falling asleep
while eating the belt at five thousand feet a minute.
In Beijing, all those too-quiet evenings,
I often found myself before the tube
watching another travelogue on Germany
with a soundtrack from Hong Kong—
        "Green Onions"
by Booker T and the M.G.s. The world is a
        small place
or so it appears to be on the small screen.
An ad would flash-cut surfing in California
to sell a computer it seemed.
Then a man in a Mao cap in a news clip
drove down the highway inside the booth of an
        electronic game,
steering an imaginary car through an imaginary city.

Thus, I often found myself watching the clouds
behind the characters on the screen
and also the hills that rise to peaks beyond
and the river that runs through that country
in one Southern Song dynasty painting
of the Columbia Gorge, a painting never made.
But, overhead, ink dots fly west
in a migrating V. Downstream,
a brush strokes the character that names the place:
a French name for stone formations,
the ones that keep appearing
the farther I am drawn into the painting.
On a clear and windy day by the river,
whitecaps spindrift while, against the cliffs,
a sailboard never comes closer or moves farther away.
Gathering my bones in a bag,
I climb a wooden stage:
an old black-and-white photograph,
                turn-of-the-century,
where natives stand on roughhewn scaffolding,
spears poised above the rapids thick
                with leaping salmon
in a river without dams, a river long passed away.
Animated to skip and skim, the sailboard
inscribes its way across the waves,
and a character is inscribed in the wake.
Planing across the surface of the poem,
I start to talk in my sleep. I leap ahead
to where I can't be. I need help

flying out of the cloud, trying to locate
and follow the ships by their sound.
Then I look down to find my hands in the dream
and there are my wings.
On the far side of the mountains
the rain keeps falling from a high sky
and turning dry before it reaches the...
Stars spread over the whole of the star quilt.
I am fifty years old, a child
inside a song of the self,
a character riding a car into the night
across a city of night, city of light...

Traveling Through Centuries

Traveling once, out on an edge,
deep in the interior, I entered
an old temple on a whim, and,
in a dim recess behind the altar,
grown thin with age,
a hanging silk banner swayed.

Bare outlines tracing once-bright colors,
a lone monk appeared to be wandering
among faded mountains and rivers.

No matter how long I looked,
no matter how long I stayed,
the question remained:

Was it rain that fell upon his sleeves
or only the threads below this world
slowly being worn away?

It Will Compose Itself

It will compose itself,
or compost itself,
in the debris of days.

"Stolen moments?"

Add a paperback romance
to the way they laugh,
a black text with a path,
and it would be a leap to ask.

Here's the scam: they have a flippancy
not so much concerned with rigors
of reason, so much as the feeling (or felling)
that the French should stick to the kiss
and the logical be limited to the poetically correct

in this theatre d'text. She has the barest
of smiles, looks slightly askance
as he glances in her direction.
Is there a reflection in the glass?
Can the filmmakers pass such a likely possibility?
Is he entering or leaving Cafe X?

There must be a trace of northwestern rain in the air,
some autumn mist that could be a tryst
for swimmers, or a way down slickened streets
to a slow boat to you-know-where.

With her, with him, time plays
a perfectly wry tune, a rune
that depicts a phrase
they will taste in their ears.

Under the Arch

Elemental or elementary,
this fool flows like a river
whenever she wanders near.
He needs a rope, a boat, or, most,
her helping hand to guide him in.
Because she drowns his sad-thrashed soul
she saves his burning skin,

and he hears any word from her
as the slightest breeze stirring
the highest sprigs in old-growth fir
or clean small streams that keep
running over the clearest sands
with the least whisper, barest murmur.
Only a passing word, an ascent, by her
might rescue and release

till he will sink and happily sink,
swimming formlessly beneath
the usual trivialities
his wide, distracted eyes must mind.
New-mown grass, mint, night-blooming jasmine

drift in scents across the bed
where this poor fool has flowed, pooled, slept,
his grateful head gladly at rest
upon her rising, falling breasts.

The Case

First he searched the cupboards
where she used to keep sweaters.
Then the suitcases up on the shelf
where clothes with half lives
sat protected, folded. He felt as though
he were going through mother's hat boxes
long ago, so light they always fell.
You can tell someone's age by the way
they are almost afraid to open drawers.
The ones below the mirror were bare
except for a few loose hairs,
a couple of broken teeth
from the comb. Each place he looked
gaped with portents of days past, a blue plateau,
or remnants of the days ahead, a cliff edge.
When you lose someone, when you are left
to look, to guess, to spin off in anger,
it is not so hard to carry the head,
stuffed with its unforgettableness,
out to the jetty's end
and throw it in the drink
with clinking cubes: unsolved, rubic.

You sit alone before the tube and swim
as detectives reel the culprits in.
They are supreme individualists,
both heroes and villains,
who can be ruthless
and still bent on the truth.
They never have to navigate the hall,
or listen to the phone
without any calls,
or fall, as we do.

Theatre d'Resurrection

The woman in question asks the man without answers to follow. They go underground and traverse a damp and shadowy region where poets go to sleep on poets' graves. Next cloud domes. Next, cutting rooms. Next, the woman leads him on a path where well-dressed people walk dots across Grand Jatte. Entering a place where sunny flowers grow by way of a ladder, the woman and the man look ahead to a bridge where 19th century locomotives blow steam that rises through the concrete of amusement parks and lifts skirts with a hiss in 1936. Taking the man across the river by way of this bridge, the woman points out the opposite shore, where a band of irregulars are fighting a uniformed company. The group triumphs, they change clothes and sides in order to keep fighting. Finally, there's a wall, and the woman calls a halt. She takes out the cock she has brought and kills it, with his help. They toss the dead cock up and over the high wall. Once the cock is across, on the other side, it crows. I wouldn't have believed it if I hadn't heard it with my own ears, he says. Maybe next time you'll believe me when I tell you, she replies.

Eros

Part miracle, part unimaginable,
he looks too small, sound asleep
under the covers of their double bed—
a tiny bald head amid rolling hills and folds of
                              star quilt
below the great headlands of their pillows.

In such a pastoral, when he gurgles
they both hear words below the surface—
the turn of streams over cobbles
and murmurs among small animals.

But when he howls, they want to shut it out.
Awakening with screams, he seems infinitely big,
the center of everything like a sun should be,

and they long again for those languid days
when they lived together in sunless space.

But now they must leap to the bidding,
to this pretty little thing
who pees upon an obliging lap
and shits upon a helpful wrist.

At 3:46 in the morning, yet,
his eyes are wide and full of life
while they shuffle, bleary and weary,
with his life to be carried
warm in a crook,
and so they are married,
tenderly hooked.

Everything Composite Is Transitory

A ball of lightning rolled to New Mexico. One small thing was about to be changed: Don Juan would become Don Quixote and all the earthworks were situated in the Great Basin, thrown down rocks to lead out into a spiral on the inland sea. Does Huck tell this? I guess. And Edmund Jaegar's total recall of plants, gulls became a likely ceremony for the wind, as would atomic tests, aunts, pins, porcupines, coyotes, smooches and the names of first husbands and wives always blurted from the lips, when you address the second.

It was a small Chinese novel, with wicked crystal holders and a small contingent of the followers of E. Y. Evans-Wentz who were practicing to be dead. Let's call the hotel the Keystone, the border town Zamora, and the fire a metaphor for the heaven-sent. Let's make a fiction of reality because no one would believe it anyway, and the denizens of the sect are mostly boulders because it is the mountain which persists and sits about sprawled in cirques, improvising one-acts for the sake of the granite cliffs.

We'll begin thirty-two miles south of Palestine
where wise men were supposed to alleviate pain
but have proven that religion generally increases it
because Palestine lies in the Bible belt of East Texas,
tight on the border of the region where Robinson
went. You remember Robinson—he was the one
pursued down the usual unlikely avenues with a
Chinese prince and Albert Camus through surf
scenes, nighttime winds and housing industries.
Robinson liked to advise building fences on Cyclone
mountain, taking poodles to Dalmatia, reading
Genesis in Port Darwin—he was quite a guy. In the
odd talk of a foursome, his name popped up like
Artaud and shock.

This leaves us in some sort of unsettled dispute
as to whether one can ascertain early warnings of an
earthquake by the behavior of animals or no.
Scientists smile as they indulge the Chinese children
once more. E.Y. winks from the wings. A
neighborhood cat races up and down the roof
overhead. Dogs howl in the dark.
It always comes in the dark, the sharp shock, a 6—
enough to bring you to its epicenter, a spiritual
essence that belongs to the local Indians, not to God.
"Leda Is Asked to Leave Paradise" falls off the
livingroom wall.

The glass is cracked all over Ilium, but Leda and her
fat swan on a long leash and the beautiful Helen,

who waits in the wings, remain unphased by such extremes as animal behavior and earthquakes.

It was a Spanish-style court—the place where Helen and I lived in the city with its code of Napoleonic bungalows and all the lives surrounding us enclosed in stucco coats with fake beams and a posturing toward the exotic. It was a sunny lemonade kind of place— bluffs above the sea—in a neighborhood full of refugees who had wandered as we had in search of dreams in our marriage, as we sat staring out at repeated sunsets and waited for the green to flash—it never did in the dark in the night in the desert when we went down into a round valley and found a flat place to sleep and awakened in the morning on the beach.

But, then, everything composite is hallucinatory. No matter where we wish to shove this thing called love, it makes meaning. Here in the attic or there in the immense square, its blank visage stands for the past and the future. Yet, to substitute love for the human condition demands just about anything at hand, including bananas, marble wrists, or dark-faced girls who roll the world on a whim off the nearest cliff, but only with the best of intentions.

I was hopin' this wouldn't become so nasty, but I can't help it. Everybody I know is a bit of a fool and so am I—what can you do? Dianetics with a dead guru?

Why not try recipes or how about sand painting—
does that sound ok? I guess. Here in California, it's
all a dream. Christmas and amnesia—
they go together like dawdles at the register. Work
out your diligence with aerobics and remember:
Each generation moves with its handcuffs securely
fastened to the class behind it. I do in fact like it,
too, when you get mean and begin to discuss the
emergent crisis in Language and Theory.

On the other hand, if you are reincarnated as a
significant other, don't blame me. Nights when the
cafes radiate despair and absinthe stirs about in the
cauldron called the cranium, the Black Virgin
unwraps the Christmas gift, the painter's insightful
gift of an ear, and down river at San Marie de la Mer,
Marie gets mixed up with a gypsy Kali and drifts out
to sea in a flaming skiff.

You'll have to excuse me. I can't keep this dial
steady. It wants to wander here and there like the
Meander River. Besides, I'm contrary. I like to note
deficiencies and then I like to remind everyone else
of theirs with great regularity. But, for instance, here
I am, and where in all of Asia Minor is the story?
O, it's true I did stand on the marble docks at
Ephesus once, and they are now twenty miles
inland—weeds where the galleys floated,
personalized license plates going to rust where
Heraclitus pissed. Do you know how much it would

cost to get one that says POETIC LICENSE?
I haven't the faintest...

In our plot, the Sage of Cuchama, Guru of the
Keystone, the late and great explicator of the Celtic
mysteries and translator of the Tibetan Book of the
Greateful Dead, falls down in his room and bumps
his head. In the resulting vision, he and his brother
wander east beyond the land of little rain on a cosmic
train to pueblo country where hill-cutting streams
tend to ravine canyons and the *español* comes back
so fast your head rolls and no matter the dip sticks,
bumper stickers, chrome rims, you fully expect to see
bullock carts passing on the roads as in the old
villages, the penitentes batting their lashes and the
ashes of copal not so far down the cordillera.

It was in Sante Fe where E.Y. appeared to be, in the
plaza where the chiefs are selling silver items and the
tourists are buying, there where the center never was
centered in the fix and the flux of muttering vacancy
and the mountains raise their plumes directly above
ski lifts. It was Sante Fe or it was the Bardo Thodol
and all the silver and turquoise jewelry belonged to
the monks in the Potola. Old, old world in New, new
world. Making it out with frozen caginess, E.Y.
babbled to smooth the various spirits, knowing full
well the miraculous vision might give up at any
second and turn into ruins—into vague signs carved
in the sky—that would whack thin air with a weird

124

warp on the wider world and all the visions unfurl in tattered prayer flag contrails!

So—E.Y. danced his way across the plaza's center stage and it was a tantric dance, an appropriation of romance, a kind of mutable stance where the soul seems to remain standing while the spirit runs rampant in the manner of U.S. Senators revamping the tax structure in Lhasa, D.C., where hands are pumped religiously and smiling golden girls ride by pact in red and white convertibles. Now the brother, whose name was Chuap, a real rock 'n' roller from Cuchama, got into his brother's act. He strutted up to the top peaks in the Sangres, and began one of his infamous rolling-in's, where, in the descent, he gathers momentum and all the political tedium that is meant to wear you away until wrong is right and right is might must get out of the way or face the amazing ball of fire.

And, as the fire came a-rolling down the mountain, gathering up various skiers, weavers, potters and other indigenous creatures (unless, of course, these Bohos had already left Sante Fe and headed south to Madrid and somewhat less expensive rents), a spotter at Los Alamos, across the Rio Grande, happened to catch a glance and signaled the Conelrad to go into effect. Thus, if you were tuned to KURR, for the latest in country 'n' western, you would be directed to tune into KUSP, for the latest in muzak and mush.

Or, if you were tuned into muzak and mush, you would be directed to KRUD, for further information. And many missiles were launched in retaliation. And they went up the mountain and Chuap grinned and ate them. And they came down from Star Wars Heaven and Chuap ducked and they struck very many roofs above very many inveterate television viewers and really upset the composition, not to say the vertical and the horizontal and the sideways as well, until *I Love Lucy* looked like hell.

The Omega

I write from an imagination
earthed in you, a wandering mind
based firmly wherever you are,
whatever you choose.
You wrote the book
and then you enclosed me
in a fable of contents
I'd only dreamed. To behold you
is to see a page appear to speak,
and a character for whom
there will never be disbelief
since the scene is set
in the perfect landscape,
and, at your address,
my restless eye cannot read,
beyond the range of your body,
anything, nothing.
It is a palimpsest of need,
so a mountain rises
beyond the word "pine"
as beyond the word "want"

a mountain is enveloped.
Who knows what could pass
crossing these peaks,
directing a life to go
in search of a lost sea
where waters appear
in the desert
to speak, and the words
make their babbling play:
a voice in a heart that contains
the haunting, riddling
measure of things,
the quiet love you bring.

Patti O'Donnell

Postcards From a California Winter

I

Hazel and amber in wordless dimension,
We see across canyons
   clear air, the movement
of quiet paws.

Winter shines silver on eucalyptus,
drops oranges on the ground.

Pomegranates split
their red pod skins,
spill seeds through yellow leaves;
the luscious waste
of thin sun on hardened grasses.

II

Spectacular chemical sunsets
glaze the stinging red orange disk
that hangs so close
to the flat sea's edge
where the yellow city ends.

III

Cold moons
     of rounded hills
Fences,
     the night runs of coyotes.

IV

The poor learn to use their eyes carefully.
Learn to look between
the crowded places, ignoring
the stains and the gridwork of wires.

Learn to look at the texture of peeling paint,
the sparkles in the asphalt,
the way the light from the gas station
shines on the leaves of the palm tree.

V

Poinsettia, the startling bloom
whose milk runs out when cut
and must be seared to stop the wound.

Poinsettia, star gathering of angles
thick with sap,
     Near palm tree glisten
         Sun December
            runs to sand.

A Rhododendron Blooming

A rhododendron blooming haunts the crossroads,
pink variance, unscented, breathes a presence.

Though I swore I'd never see her,
the one who might have been
appears on the other side of choices,
and I watch her, too.
Her face my other reflection, my silences her voice.

It's the midpoint, the fulcrum, a difficult time;
what was, and what will be, a fusion of channels.

Traipsing across the street, and up it and down
      to show the neighbors—
snapshots, testimonials—
a new way of walking to a new world, grown.

And all the while that world was shifting
beyond 41st Street and pink net formals...

Honey, jam, date stickiness
a little tea, a little toast,
figs, raisins, the clucking of tongues,
strong fingers on fat aprons.

"So, so, a bite to eat for Ainy, some for Patty,
here, I picked a rosebud for the two little buds."

Then the analyst left, and all the cats
ran into the other room,
created by the grandmother
whose left-handed stitches were hard to learn.

The pink net formal's gone into the trunk.
Its artificial flowers fade as surely as their models,
but it's taken years.

…fragments…picked one image at a time
from the antigravity of an outward space,
the falling of apples…
It is the orchard, and it's autumn.

Lyric Suite

I

Out of the torpor
of the white lit afternoon
a music rises in the pepper tree,
hits the roses,
disturbs a bird.

A singing whistle is somewhere released,
the bird complains on the wire.

A.M.–F.M. on the radio dial—
all possibility surfaces
kandi-appled, metal flaked,
heat gleams flashing.

Minor dissonance:
a train,
        chit chit chit chit
the mocking bird and the plane overhead—

a skyful of noise moves in and out of
a compact density.
Inside the wood box room
the pressure is astounding.

Outside, a butterfly
thinks he is Mozart;
white wings, the intricacies of air.

Earlier, hearing the music,
a look would have been exchanged.
What is lacking now
is the willingness
to entertain its implications,

remembering lost perfections:
pink trees, white clouds and piano keys
crossing campus to the music lesson,
interpretations of the measure
practiced to further subtlety.

II

There should be roses on the piano,
a spread of leaves in all voices,
dancing cells of all color,
a shawl
silk and fringy in Spanish flowers,
the play of cats on the table.

Aquarium, siren, and continuum, a
splash of rain,
and an almost silence

like a Torrey Pine,
like sunshine on stucco,
or the freeway at 3:00 A.M.

136

III

There should be dice to throw,
a canvas to act upon,
Art
splashed gold all about us,
moving in the numbers game
we play every day of our lives.

Gasoline and taxes, the price of food,
what's actually there in the cupboard
weighed against
the time block we find ourselves in.

The part and particle of matters,
the zones we rent, the
parking space available,
the changing colors of streetlights and clouds,
the long and the short of shadows.

The wind,
calling us out
to whatever expectations we may find
once entering traffic:

colors moving quadrilaterally,
the promises of sunny afternoons.

Chance meetings,
the astonishments
of time,
a skimmering of marbles,
orbits of ropes,

childhood constructing self
in childhood's image,
the yellow balloon on the freeway
improbably crossing unharmed.

Urban Nocturne

The moment is tangible
as a noun makes it so, but
moving the hand through air
it stays on the other side,
will not be grasped outside of extension:
the lion's roar,
the peacock's reply
from the other side of the canyon.

In random composition comes
the train, the dogbark,
blues
on the neighbor's stereo,
the smell of skunk
and a possum in the kitchen.

Gears shift in the sky.

One after another
their screaming ascents
break up the atmosphere,
shatter the clouds.

In the rapping combustion of metal wings
the heavens change
and a whistle mourns for them.

Moving
        face in the window
My own?

The whistle scares me,
trains
go by so fast, and

the pulse
        that stops a plane or

picks up a leaf

is random
        as the wind
                chimes…

The invisible,
caught in periphery,
turning—

a scampering of air
and the watcher vanishes
into the cracks
night brings to the windows.

From the Language Cage

I

The rose
whose power to move us
rests now in
the thing itself
and not the word
must be surprised to be so naked.

The cross, the
sword, the coin
have all gone under.
Tongues
are uprooted, still
nothing's changed but our insistence
on new images.

New hearts
to tick to an
atomic clock

and

what kind of sound
do clocks make in French?

I said,
"I don't even want to hear
about Paderewski's
practice methods," but
he told me anyway,
and now
it's morphemes and their composites
ticking off the chatter.

Andante
        on Dante,

the spiral

descends to the language cage
outside of which

we gesture vaguely
from our separate jungles.

II

At the point where all rules stop
the ear begins
its assimilations...

connections link themselves
to the soundtrack which
must, somehow, we think,
be linear: a solid mechanic
of the projectionist,
the square light at
the back of the theater

reminding us it's
a movie we're watching, not
the real thing
        at all,

not

        a horse
any more than
the word
        is a horse,

not

like the afternoon in Ensenada
when the cow pony you were riding
slipped into the herd of longhorns—

dust, and spike-haired, pock-marked,
fly-infested smells that
finally focused on the saddle horn, the
reins, and the coarse black hair
on the back of the neck
of your horse
that afternoon in Ensenada,

not
that kind of horse,

this time
it's a different entity.

Outside Utopia

I

In Twentieth Century alleyways
the blonde haired child
with hand-picked flowers
walks blithely by construction beams
and drills that crack the sidewalk
where she steps.

Dead ends and city blocks,
around the corner another street
as strange as an empty warehouse.
Green streetlamps light
the building site, earthmounds,
excavations.

In the spaced-out skeleton
of emerging structure,
a petrified energy
pervades the silence
where suddenly
it's eerie
to be alive.

II

Spare ice and chrome,
an exercise
in spoons and tortured cellos.
Should one believe the geek?
Souls twisted in acrylic
haunt the penthouse.

Across the city
at a corner store
abandoned a year ago
tomato cans explode,
fish multiply…

Order
is an agreement,
the line a painting on the ground

on either side of which
the propositions
arch like MacDonald's
in neon over asphalt

where the cars
stop and go.

Positive—Negative
and the force between fields
where still grow
the lilacs,
bush, grass, and berries.

Untitled Spring

The newsboy in the city
on a deserted Sunday
pulls his wagonload of headlines
down the hill.

He has a cane to help him up again,
to pull the empty wagon rattle clack,
tap clatter rattle clack,
tap rattle clatter clack,

up through the Sunday streets
through the dawn's gray asphalt,
through the sleeping city
rattle clack,
tap clatter rattle clack.

It is Spring.

Does he see the red rhododendron
spread semicircle like a fan
strutting home this morning
like a streetwalking peacock?

Chase down the ages,
the myths will not let go,

though we hardly see them
through our laminated bindings.

When there does come a spring
of real forsythia, lilac,
we're
      left dumb by it.

Turning in the middle
we strike a pose,
cannot admit
      the miracle;

insist upon abstractions
between ourselves and flowers.

The last time I was alive,
five sparrows flew at dawn,
crossed wires, and kept on flying
past all the telephone poles,
gaggling in a chestnut tree
that could hardly contain
the noise of them.

In and out of the air they went
following currents for the flow.
Observing, recording,
I stood and watched
      almost,
            almost as long.

Branch hush, warm

cool shadow rustle
playlight, sunshade, quiver!
Quick the bird-song wing,
the gray brown,
feather dappled
twig.

Friday Afternoon at the Zoo

Up on the deer mesa
where everything is placid,
the unicorn sits silent,
Darwin's Rhea blinks its eyes.
Roan oryx came to visit,
Giraffe Child meditated,
the Dragon Tree, the Olive,
Firethorn bramble traveled fast.

There was a daisy field
of spotted deer, and zebra colts
and prancing, an eye-beam cross
at the llama's pen,
and a downwind stench.

Bamboo moon marks bore graffiti,
the map showed me the way
down past the yak and North Plains Bison,
feathers in my eyes,
past the Ostrich, eucalyptus grove

to Typhon Cape—Red-Eye,
the Buffalo of Water
who could not stare me
down nor hear
the Eagle fly on Friday
or see
the lion roaring anyhow.

Emily, Sometimes You Scare Me

A poem for Olde Witch

A single seat at the back of the theatre,
the laundromat at 10:00 P.M.,
afford an "out of it"
view from the bridge
game, but
I hate it when things get too official.

How did the red coin purse enter?
And is it here to stay?

Evenings spent
learning to play "Meadowlands"
on the balalaika—learning
to play anything on the balalaika,
including how to tune it—

the door an outrageous
mouth and a wink,
daffodils for remembrance,

these are a few of my
favorite things, but
played
the way Coltrane
adds the truth.

151

Where the Music Ends

In memory of Miles Davis

We hug to ourselves the memory of it,

keep the flight path
    in our minds

and fix a point mid-heaven

that resounds in space
beyond our ears, the
bone expanded to include
what's almost getting out of it—

      the lyric
      the song
         the summons
         to the singing places

Space
  is necessary

to the twelve-tone scale,

the steppes   stretch open

the chord   the mode   the note

whose harmonies

      throw colored hoops
      to ring the sun god's nest.

Speed, too, will dazzle
like ks-and-ts-and-qs distinctly distant.

Circles of fours,
circles of fives
augment, diminish
to the last
        thin
          reed.

What's left is the echo

        chromatic,   illusive,

so cold
in reflective radiance
its questions.

Bonnie Rosecliffe

Surprised by Morning

Light seeps through the curtain,
watery, gray as a dim ocean.
We lift our heads
and fall back into deep slumber.

Outside now the birds, delirious, begin
incessant song. We smile
in our sleep at their imperfect notes,
trilled for just another day.

When did it come to this? We hide
away from day, beneath the pillow.
Pull the blankets up around us,
stalling the moment of arising.

We, who began our days with a cry,
a smile, coo, or warbled song.

Outburst, 5:00 A.M.

The dawn has brought its early light
to slip through slatted blinds.
Almost jailed in my pink cocoon
I rouse from wary dreams.

All night I've planted
cosmos, daffodils, hyacinth
on soldiers' unmarked graves.
But my brother will not shut up.
I joined the Marines in '68!
I'm a dead man!
Cannon fodder, that's what!
My dream flowers won't root in sand.
My brother does not stay buried.
Often, at dawn, like Jacob's angel,
he wrestles with me. TV gunfire.
Sometimes he begs for a story—
A house so safe, Robbie,
nobody can hurt us.
He peels back his shredded heart.

In my arms, he bleeds to death.
I might just tell him

it's all a dream.
He'll soon wake up.
But he's gone,
sucked behind
enemy lines.
I crawl from bed,
walk on my knees
to the blue lady of mercy,
surrendering,
demand an end
to this.

The Dream Is Love

After surgery
I dream someone watches.
My mother finds his prints.
He looked through
the window at me
drugged against
the pain.
He could hold a knife.
My mother sweeps
his prints away.
She locks the doors
and windows
pulls the blinds
and stays close by.
If I could hear the man
as he pressed his mouth
to the window,
he'd say, "Trillium
along the creek."
He'd say he watched over
my struggle to breathe

and stayed when I burned
with scarlet fever.
"Let me cool you
with this water,
a melt of snow."
I hear him
in the bushes
as they rustle.
If he'd take
my mother on his lap,
he'd hold her
in her light blue dress
or tear it from her shoulder.
He'd soothe her forehead
and tell her
he's my angel
or my own
fierce will
to live.

Just As

(Desert Storm, 1991)

A raw wind.
Winter red grass
in a dry creek bed.
Granite tilts up
to tree roots
twisted into the hill.
Patches of snow-crust
melt. The ground
gives way to early spring.
Worn by street noise, the news of war,
we yield to this meadow
and run like children
holding out our arms
like aeroplane wings,
gliding into each other,
and laughing, embrace.
Just as now, perhaps, shrapnel
splinters the bone,
just as, now, perhaps
an Iraqi woman covers the ears of her child,
just as a soldier with cracked shoes
loads his rifle.
Mist eases up the slope.
Pines tremble in a wisk of wind.

Bhajan

Where have you hidden my sorrow, beloved?

I've taken your basket of stones,
and left you mangoes, a flute.

But who will sing for me
when you go away?

I never leave you
(or so he says),
for I come to you wanting
as you do me.

I hear your words,
but I have seen you
with the woman
who dances with fire.
I know it was you
I saw with her.

I breathe in you
like your only song.
Is not your heart beating
in the palm of my hand?

Yes, and my tongue
in your mouth
seems to take root.
As your mouth opens to universes,
vines break from stones.
Hold me, hold me.
I want to carry your scent,
not jasmine and air,
but your own lotus blue sweat.
God, I want
your scent on my skin.

Polishing the Silver

At the window, I watch
wind tumbling mustard
in the field out back,
a meadow of cheat grass.
June. But that wind's
still blowing cold
down from the Three Sisters.
They shiver in clouds
like sheer white blouses
above the pine ridge.
June, so I polish the silver.
With a flannel cloth
I rub pink paste
into scrolled silver roses
and wonder at my blurred face
in the spoon's rounded back.
My hair's still dark.
This mirror doesn't show my worry.
The worry's in my hands,
veins twisted and knotting,
my skin chapped and red.

I rub tarnish from plates
my eldest used to polish.
She still sends flowers
pressed between white paper.
Queen Anne's lace & pansies,
their blossoms thin as butterfly wings,
the paper dusted with pollen.
Sometimes I want to write
My days are lonely
with your father gone.
Instead I write I'm polishing silver.
Out on the ridge
I pick her wild flax:
break the stem
sky blue petals
fall.

No Stone God

No stone god
can claim me,
nor the virgin
in her cape of stars.
Not the god
with tongues of fire.
I bow to none.
Those images of Jesus
in his crown of thorns
do not move me.
I swear by no holy books.
I invoke no sacred name.
I call you by a name
known only to you.
Tonight you're my gray wool shawl.
I wrap you around me
and sit by the fire
to mourn my lost children.

Piece for Two Hands

Midlife I find my hands surprise.
My hands are small, the span short,
but just in time I learn again
the touch of ivory. Already dusk?
I bow as if before an altar
to strike a deep regard for hands.
"Without pride" Satie scores
the phrase where fingers touch a blue
so soft the sea would merge with sky.
Sainted blue: the final chord
pianissimo, the bells unmeasured tremble.
Divested, I kneel beside a fount
and bathe my hands in holy water.

The Limits of Language
(or the uses of words)

Words can be like spoons and used to scoop out cantaloupes of meaning. As hands, words will pat and knead meaning like bread dough. However, words are not simply useful in the kitchen, the culinary approach.

Words are also useful in traveling, especially words like "meraviglia" or "Smetterlink," German for butterfly.

One might conceivably say this word on a walk through a meadow if one happened upon such a bright-winged thing.

Words can be shaded. The meaning may depend upon one's background. One person told us that the first time he heard the word "nuance," he thought it meant something new, like a style.

If words are shaded, shapely, and useful, in this theory of language, they may resemble trees. In fact, Robert Graves speaks of a tree-alphabet. In this elaborate code, one can wander through entire forests of language.

Interlude. It would be nice to have some music here…something clean without much verbiage. One thing bothersome about words is the aspect of referents. This can be played upon with scat cat drap baaraatlap shebam kebam baby talk dooodooodooodoogeep. Sometimes I just like to float around without landing anywhere, without attaching myself, a spider sailing out on a lengthy thread—no more like a word seeking a referent, a lichen gripping a stone.

Some words, of course, are difficult to categorize. Spindrift, curlicue, overboard, schabamm, pizzazz, sequin, derring-do, and deviltry. Mephistopheles takes a powder. She destroyed the garden and the whole house, too. Entire sentences can be composed, reverences revoked.

Language breathes. It transcends its use. It takes on its own life. When you want to go to sleep, it won't shut up. Language keeps on yapping, quibbling. It'll quarrel and spin yarns all night.

In some comic strip, the poet shouts, "Shut up!" He turns to his wife, "Honey, I can't sleep. The words won't stop." His wife, a musician-painter says, "You think you have problems. Indigo was playing the shakahashi just now, and I'm missing the program." In the last frame, God laughs, big-bellied, and shouts: "Language is no curse!!"

The poet, obedient, repeats some three-word
voiceless prayer. A cry goes up. Release me, Spirit,
from this necessity. Language calls upon me now to
speak another tongue. I come clean with blood and
snow. Oh, live within me, healing wordless fire.

Blackbird

It wasn't until I was older that my mother told me that Norma had a breakdown because she saw her father-in-law kill a man with an axe. She was in the same room when he chopped him to bits.

Norma had married a serviceman and moved to Michigan right after the war. Norma didn't know her husband very well. She didn't even know he had been married before until after they said their vows. "Her husband was a real jerk," my mother said. While Norma was married, she had to wait on her father-in-law hand and foot.

Norma had been such a beautiful child that her mother didn't let her do anything. She didn't ask her to set the table, wash the dishes, or sweep the floors. She wouldn't let her go out and climb trees or play much with other children. She didn't let her do a thing for herself. Norma was raised to be taken care of.

After the murder, when Norma went insane, her parents went to Michigan and brought her and the baby home, back to Rochester. Norma lived with her mother and father, my Great-Aunt Mary and my Uncle Tobias, until my Aunt Mary died. She was in and out of the New York State Mental Hospital. The New York State Mental Hospital was a place I used to get confused with the prison. Both were made of brick and had barred windows.

One time we went to visit the family in their small apartment, Norma was having a spell. She lay in a dark room with the shades pulled down. Only a slit of light came through a crack between the shades and the window. She looked small, her face troubled and dark, as she lay under a satin comforter in the wide bed. A picture of Jesus was above her on the wall, his red heart glowing. He looked as if he longed to wash her in his blood.

Norma didn't say anything to us that day. She lay there with her eyes wide open. My Aunt Mary tried to get her to talk to my mother. "Here's Betty," she said gently. "Honey, you remember Betty." But Norma didn't say anything. She tried to smile a little, a troubled, troubling smile. Then she pulled the sheet over her face.

We left the room then and Norma lying in the wide bed. In the living room, we sat on the maroon over-stuffed couch with the doilies tacked on the arms. My Aunt Mary served us tea and vanilla wafers. I

173

perched on the edge of the davenport, my legs itching from the scratchy couch. Darlene, Norma's daughter, stared at me.

Darlene, two years younger than me, didn't look like a child. She always wore dresses and looked like a little old lady with hair down to her waist. Her lips were dark with Real Red lipstick.

My other cousins, the silly cousins, made fun of her when we were at my grandmother's house. At the Christmas parties we used to play cancan girls and giggle and laugh while we jumped around and swished our skirts back and forth, lifting our petticoats to show our panties. But Darlene never danced with us. She always hung back a little, with her braid in her mouth.

She was staring at me now, with her braid in her mouth. I didn't know what to say to her.

But she spoke first. "Do you want to see the bird?" she asked. "Do you want to see the blackbird?"

"Sure," I nodded.

We got up and went to the back of the apartment. She slept in a small curtained-off cubbyhole behind the kitchen. Not much to her room. Just a bed with a crocheted afghan, a lot of dolls, and a shelf full of books, like *The Jungle Book* and *Kidnapped*. She had told me to read *Kidnapped*, but I never did.

On a small table at the end of her bed was a cage. And in it a large black bird.

I remembered then I had already seen it. "Oh, I remember...you had him down at the lake last summer."

We had gone to visit them when they were camping at Vine Valley. Smiling, almost radiant, Norma had shown us the baby starling with a broken wing. She had bandaged the wing and kept the bird in a cage. I thought it was very messy and made strange sounds. But today the cage was clean, and the bird just sat there, opening and closing its beak, but making no sound. It looked at me with one bright, hard eye.

"Is it still hurt? Does it still have a broken wing?"

"I don't know. I think it might be better," Darlene smiled at me, a sad smile, like the smile of her grandmother.

Somehow, I wanted to like Darlene. I wanted to be friends with her. I wanted to show her the shining places on the creek near my house and share my favorite cowrie shells with her and tell her stories with happy endings. Or I wanted to want to.

"I like your hair," I said.

She smiled. "My grandma says there's so much you can do with long hair. You should try growing yours long."

Darlene told me all the things she could do with her hair—pull it back in a ponytail, twist it up, make loops and baskets, wear it in a long braid. I pulled at my just-below-the-ears cut and said, "Yeah, I think I'll grow mine long…like yours…Can I brush your hair?"

She stood at the end of the bed then, and I sat on it to brush her long soft brown hair. I brushed it softly and gently, the way my mother brushed mine. I went into a daze, brushing her hair, just like when my mother brushed mine. I didn't think about anything, just her soft brown hair, like a river.

Darlene's shoulders shook a little. She started crying. She sank beside me on the bed and said, "Will you be my friend? I don't have any friends."

I looked at her, stunned. Her face all bunched up as she tried to hold the tears back. She was gulping in huge sobs.

I patted her a little on her back. I nodded, I could only nod. The blackbird just sat in his cage, silent, unsinging. Something I had done, I thought, something I had done had made her cry.

Her grandma came in then and sat with her, rocking Darlene in her arms. I looked on for a while and then went out to the living room. My mother looked worried. "We should go," she said. "Before it gets dark."

My mother went to the back of the house. I heard her saying goodbye to my great-aunt and Darlene. I couldn't hear Darlene crying anymore. Just Aunt Mary's soft voice.

I walked with my mother downstairs and out to the car. The street was black, lined with icy ridges of snow.

On the way home, I asked my mother, "What's wrong with Norma? What's wrong with Darlene's mother?"

"She's sick," my mother said. "She has a mental illness. She can't help it. She's just sick. She just gets these spells. Someday when you're older I'll tell you more."

We drove in silence through the twilight. Next time I saw Darlene, I thought, maybe I could talk her into letting that bird go. But, then, I thought, what about Norma? What would she do without the blackbird? Last summer she used to sit by it and sing, "Blackbird, blackbird, have you no wings?" I curled up next to the car door and thought about how to make things right.

Now I am grown, the blackbird, like my Aunt Mary and my uncle, has long since died in captivity. In a recent family photo, Norma looks shy, dark, heavy. Darlene stands beside her mother, her long hair tied back, a young woman in an old woman's dress. And me? I'm standing with the cousins who used to laugh the most, before they married men who beat them. Do you see me? My hair is short. I look out at the camera with large, almost wondering eyes. I'm the one in the middle, trying hard to smile.

Kate Watson

Caterpillars in Hawk Canyon

1

A landslide of caterpillars
tumbling in the dust in Spring:
some slim, some fatter.

They slip and spill
from lip of rock
to curling leaf
and scatter,
somersaulting downside up
in desert sand; some
land happily
and munch on greens;
some stumble
into spider traps;
others scramble
backwards
up the rockface
to the place
where chrysalises
wag in the wind.

2

Through the summer
a drove of editors
our footing loose
are of a sudden
out of sedentary work
and falling over one another
in our shared predicament;
some of us will spiral into panic,
others thrive on serendipity
and some will learn the trick
of keeping steady
as we plod on,
deep down believing
in the promise of wings.

The Depression, 1931

Maybe a chill wind teased and licked
the curtain; maybe on a table by the stair
a teacup rattled; but I'm sure there was
no music, not on that morning when he
hung in the bedroom of his English home.
No gallows trap; but the drop got the job done.
I don't know who found him, cut the cord
of his dressing-gown, closed his eyes
and laid him down, silent, still warm
on the crumpled sheets. His wife?
One of his three sons, the youngest
only twelve? The village nurse, who
visiting the sickroom knocked as usual
and thought he must be sleeping?

Barren spring: foul play against him
exacerbating failure, along with others,
he went under. Illness followed,
and long fevers left his body frail.
Was he in rage against the dwindling light,
or did panic fret behind his eyes as he sensed
the abyss writhe and rise to tug him in?

Did he sink half-weeping into suffocation,
fright and agony a mixture as confused
as tears and sweat? Or did he amble into death,
he already part ghost, and death not an ogre
but an opening, offering a water-soft embrace?

The Immigrants:
Where the Roots Grow

We come with our roots attached.
They dangle between our legs like seaweed;
they cling to our noses and our knees.
We're holding fast to the ladder
but the next rung is worn through—
it's a long way to heaven
but we're coming as we can,

as we can: carrying the dream
through the weight of our years
through the weight of the onslaught
of abundance. Machines and glitter.
Our lips can move only as fast
as our stomachs are filled
in the brief interval
before darkness.

Love is your best bet.
If you want us to thrive,
reach us like a wind current, curving;
win us like the roots of a tree do the soil,
curling under, and spreading.
We'll suck the sweet earth and bring you music.
We'll do so willingly
because this is our home.

Boundaries

My grip tightens and you snap shut,
catching me fast in a snare
that cripples and burns.
It will work only when we both agree
to come and go without clutching;
when we learn to ease apart
into separate selves;
when I may also enter you,
may move through the corridors
that open onto your rooms.

We have stayed faithful
through many absences
but now I'm tired of shadowdancing.
I've been stuck here long enough
guarding our storm-tossed flame,
grasping at smoke plumes
that spiral, then die.

When I call I never know
if this time you'll be a person
or a wall. When the wall is up

I wish the clowns would roll in
or the cats acting real cool,
sidling past, their tails high;
only the beggar is there
stammering, choking on brick.

If we're to reach each other
you must risk the crossing, too.

I haven't forgotten
how your body fits with mine,
boundaries dissolving
in crucible, in steaming swamp.
I haven't forgotten—
crimson flower, throbbing stem
throbbing flower, crimson stem
        flowering stem.
Your tongue's milk sweetens me;
I line my womb for you
with petals chosen one by one.

Don't you know it hurts
when you close so suddenly?
We are by nature porous.
Neither one of us
can thrive inside stone.
I'm going to squeeze free.
I'll slip inside the wind,
you'll see.

Trinity

She meets I
in the body
which is one
with my mother

I can see
where she sits by the blue fire
flame-quick knitting
Is she sighing
shall I sing
she is I
am a long way away
when the wind blows

white wall coal black
light grey hair

my mother winks
from the middle of the flame
and I rise up
and leave her
alone
In the fire a reflection

come home?

The Clachan

Scots: The Village

Galloway in Springtime.
Black-faced lambs and wet mud
and the wind in our hair.

Slip out
the back door, past
the ash bucket,
tread gingerly
down steps that are mucky
and slippery with lichen,
with last night's frost.

Over the knoll and down in the valley
sedges grow along the edge of the burn
as it trickles over pebbles
with a tinkling sound.
The ground, quickening,
stirs beneath our bellies
as we stretch, dipping hands
to trap tadpoles in a jar.

✱   ✱   ✱

A crackle on lilac
is how it starts:

spitting, maybe stopping at a drizzle,
maybe driving hard, thudding on the rooftops,
plopping, plopping, dripping from the eaves,
from the leaves of the apple tree,
drops hung like pearls on the wild rose.

*   *   *

Now daylight lasts into evening,
ice cream drips from the cone
and the river beckons.

We set out at a saunter,
happy to dawdle down the dirt path,
plucking here and there a spear of grass
to chew—juice tasting sweet between our teeth.

Amble on, mindful of the Covenanters'
graves behind the church wall,
teaching us what *persecution*
means—and *martyr*, and *long ago*.

Let's run, race, fast as we can,
spring down the grass bank, fly
till a stitch in the side
stops us short and we stand
entranced, the chatterdance
of water fixing us in a stare.

*   *   *

Gobstoppers. Lollipops.
Licorice sticks, chocolate drops,

lovehearts and luckybags,
toffee, cooled in a tray,
shattered by a hammer,
sixpence worth in a paper poke.

James the Fourth was a good king,
so we learn; and we learn to sit up straight,
to wait our turn to speak
and not to cheek the teacher
when her back is turned. We learn
the sting of leather on our hands.

                 *   *   *

Nippy. Shiver a bit.
The souch of the wind
lifts and skirls
around Earlstoun Loch.
Farmers labor after dark,
bringing in the hay
before the weather breaks.

The village has measles,
mumps, impetigo,

and the young MacLean lad—
from along the road—
has died of asthma.

Wood; water; stone.

                 *   *   *

Here's the butcher's van
and the man himself—all
bloodied from the meatcuts,
happy as a top
selling prime beef, meat pies,
fresh baps and Sunday roast—
honking the horn up the hill,
signaling the housewives
to form a queue,
glad of a chance to blether.

Raw cold and long nights
tether us at home.
We gather by the hearth
feed our dreams to the fire,
tell of an ermine we saw,
and are silent,
living in books.

Outside,
snow is falling,
softer than moths' wings.

Smudge

Pussycat,
pink-eared, squints
in the sunshine,
sniffing flowers.

Button-eyed, she
purrs and
furlicks my legs
in the kitchen.

Four years ago, four
kittens, born
in a drawer, smelled
of a barnyard.

Mature, she sleeps
in a circle,
the slope of her head
suggests—young doe.

The Waterfall

Later I would climb
and hear in the valley
the sounds of Malinalco:
school bells, a cutting saw,
grate and scrape,
car horns, wind on tin,
the mild flat cacophony of animals
in farmyards and far off through fields.

Now, the village air squeaks
with bird song. Early yet.
On cobbled ground,
rose and grey stone church
nearby, a mother—mocha colored,
red bandanna bound
round long black hair—
beckons me to come. Smiling.
A baby cradled in her arms.
Nut-brown mite, maybe five,
half-hides between the folds
of her mother's skirt.
Mule-jawed woman.

Baby.
Baby in
her arms in
my arms
now.

Snatches I understand—
Señora, por favor...
cuide a la niña...
no tiene a nadie—

She's begging me
to take the baby,
and her words, reaching in,
find the waterfall
that longs to nourish
something young.

Heavy, wrapped
in a shawl, sleeping.
Sun strong on our faces.
I shake my head,
hand back the child.
—Are you hungry?
Here, I have bread.
Your daughter's eyes
are large, black grapes
in the sun.

A Patient Master

Late afternoon in Morelia.
About the town
the sand-pink stone
emanates a blend
of prayer and pleasure.

Hushed
against a darkening sky,
the cathedral
is a patient master.

Rain bursts abruptly
and batters the streets
till the gutters run.

Young folk
scatter in a panic,
scurrying under archways
for cover.

On the corner,
one old man
scarcely moves:

Underneath a huge sombrero,
chiseled stone
in the pouring rain,
the lone figure
ties down plastic
over corn and papaya,
fastens his overcoat
button by button
and stands, by his cart,
quite still.

Into Silence

In memory of Owen Kane

To a body anything can happen
        —George Oppen

Owen laughing:
driving through the city on daily rounds
with trays of wheatgrass and alfalfa;
cheerful in his work and curious,
he stops now and then for a gossip
with friends;
        Spring pushes through,
sticky and smelly and wondrous with blossom,
and Owen is busy as ever,
a busy man in the lap of life.

I know him by the things he loves—
like Marcia's voice,
Melissa's fingers on the strings,
the silly side of pageantry—
his delight in dressing for a show
in stripy braces and the brightest mustard vest.

I know him through his poetry,
grown and plucked with a gardener's hand.

Owen plummets into silence.
Like a brick.
We wait: the lips and arms of his friends.
Midnight. City fidgets.
Thunder makes rocks in an angry sky.
Owen is a tree, stricken.

We gather near him in coma
reading Whitman at 1:00 A.M.,
crooning fragments of hymns and lullabies;
nurses tuck and adjust, check
and record; days blur into nights
without pause—many weeks pass.

Summer grass
mown and heaped.

Eros lingers, a little,
in the dancing of one hand
and in his hair.

For a Refugee Boy Blinded
by Shelling in Bosnia

(April 1993)

He can see nothing,
and yet even for his sake
the guns have not gone silent.
Now his hands must lead,
his fingertips, flimsy in air,
feeling for contours
they recognize: a doorjamb,
the curve of a mirror,
somewhere he calls home.

But he has no home,
no familiar geography.

He has the blood and grime
of war, crack of rifle fire,
crush of limbs in a truck
as it bumps and stumbles
through the Bosnian night;

a hospital bed
in a city he'll never see.

Eyes wrapped
in lint and gauze,
he braves the dark:
shoulders
curl in, feet take
little steps, the head
shies away as though
   from a
 bright light,
too bright,
   as though
 anticipating
some blow.

Solo

I take the freeway and highway down
past ploughed land
alongside willow
on beyond blue Otay lakes.
Marsh makes the shrubs here lush:
when dust subsides
I'm high on pollen.

It's on the ride up my nerves writhe.
Five plus the pilot
in a plane for four.
Wowee! I sit knees up, tongue clutching lip,
no thing between me
and the speckled purple hills
miles below me.

First to go, I'm in the door, legs out—
they blow like paper.
Jump! Arch—Count through free fall,
and my canopy has blossomed.
Safely adrift in the luxury of sky
I steer my way landward
on an easy wind.

About the Poets

Richard Astle, having ancestors at Runnymede, at Culloden and on the Pony Express, is an age mate of DeNiro, Deneuve, Dresman and O'Donnell. Born in Kentucky, raised in Shaker Heights and schooled in California, he has worked as a paperboy, postman, musician, teacher and programmer in Cleveland, San Francisco, Los Angeles and San Diego. Richard acknowledges no influence, or any. He lives in Del Dios with his wife and their cat, takes walks by the lake and writes when he has to. "The Decay of the Vacuum" has previously been published in *Crawl out Your Window.*

Sarai Austin was born on a farm in Missouri along the banks of the Mississippi River; she has lived most of her adult life in California. Her work emerges from the tale-telling tradition of the rural mid-South and is created largely for oral performance.

Ted Burke, born 1952 in Detroit, Michigan, has lived in San Diego since 1969. A 1983 graduate of the University of California at San Diego literature department, he has written for the *Reader, San Diego Door* and *Kicks,* and has had

his poetry anthologized in *Ocean Hiway: 8 Poets in San Diego* (Wild Mustard Press, 1982). He cites his main influences as Bob Dylan, T. S. Eliot and Frank O'Hara. He lives and writes in San Diego.

Peter Dragin was born and raised in Cleveland, Ohio. When his big sister went to college, she left behind some *Evergreen Reviews,* and thus Peter took his first poetic nourishment. Learning and friendship are what he enjoys best. He studied religions and classical and oriental languages at San Diego State University for two decades. He reads his work when invited and has published in *Ocean Hiway: 8 Poets in San Diego,* and in the self-published *Slim Hymns.* He lives with his cat.

Paul Dresman, who was born (1943) and raised in Southern California, moved north to attend San Francisco State University in 1965: many remarkable teachers, including Kai-yu Hsu. He completed his MA thesis in 1970, and was a CO during the third Asian war in his lifetime. Later, at the University of California at San Diego, he wrote his PhD dissertation on Edward Dorn and "history" (1980). In 1986, he was invited to teach at Beijing Normal University by the Chinese woman poet, Zheng Min. He currently lives with his wife and two sons in Eugene, where he teaches at the University of Oregon.

Bonnie Rosecliffe teaches English at Mesa College in San Diego. Her purpose in writing is to keep still while moving. For her, the poem, especially, is something like a recreational vehicle (poem as RV). She enjoys being published in the company of friends. Some of these poems have appeared in *Dream International Quarterly.*

Patti O'Donnell, a native San Diegan, has also lived in the Northwest. She has given numerous readings in Southern California and been published in several literary magazines, including *Maize,* where "Untitled Spring" first appeared. Patti has served the community by running a reading series for the San Diego Historical Society, and she was also active in a project that produced a half-hour television program for KPBS on border poets.

Kate Watson grew up in Dalr Kirkcudbrightshire, a country village in the southwest of Scotland. She studied French Somerville College, Oxford, f two years and holds a lit/writi degree from the University of California at San Diego. Whi UCSD, she helped catalog th books and tapes in the Archiv New Poetry. For the past seve years she has worked in publis Her poems have appeared in and in the anthology *Voices in Struggle for Peace and Justice.*